Intellectual Property Rights - 1

OrangeBooks Publication

1st Floor, Rajhans Arcade, Mall Road, Kohka, Bhilai, Chhattisgarh - 490020

Website: **www.orangebooks.in**

© Copyright, 2024, Author

All rights reserved. No part of this book may be reproduced, stored in a retrieval system, or transmitted, in any form by any means, electronic, mechanical, magnetic, optical, chemical, manual, photocopying, recording or otherwise, without the prior written consent of its writer.

First Edition, 2024

Intellectual Property Rights - 1

Dr. Rakesh Ainapur
Adv. Radha Chaudhary

OrangeBooks Publication
www.orangebooks.in

Index

1. Introduction To IPR 1
2. Patents 11
3. Trademark 47
4. Cyber Intellectual Property 82
5. Geographical Indications 116
6. International Convention and Treaties 144
7. Bibliography 166

Introduction to IPR

> **Introduction to IPR**
>
> Overview of the concept of property; Industrial Property and Non-Industrial Property; Historical background of IPR; Importance of Human Creativity in present scenario; Different forms of Intellectual Property and its conceptual analysis.
>
> Summary-Questions from previous year question papers.

Introduction

Intellectual Property Right has occupied critical place in the ever-changing modern business world, which is characterized by innovation, modern designs, and global operations. Protecting intellectual property in this open wide world is a challenging task for innovators and business houses. Especially post information technology revolution, where most of the business happens through internet, which is an anonymous platform, infringement of Intellectual Property is very common. This chapter is structured to cover - Concept of property and its types, concept of intellectual property and types, and historical development in the field of intellectual property area.

Property

Property is one which can be owned by individual, corporation or any legal person and enjoy the end-to-end rights related to property - sell, improve, lease, earn from the asset, or destroy the asset. These properties can be classified into - Tangible and Intangible properties.

Tangible properties are typically physical assets or property owned by a company, such as equipment, buildings, inventory, and others. These assets are used to produce their product and services. These can be of two types - Movable assets (Eg. Vehicles, Machinery etc) and non-movable assets (Eg. Land and Building).

Intangible Properties are non-physical assets of a company which have a monetary value but not physical existence. These are considered as properties since it will have potential revenue generating capability. Intangible property can be of two types, namely Industrial Property and Non-Industrial Property. Industrial properties are concerned with factory and business whereas non-industrial properties are concerned with artistic work, author, and other human skills.

The rights of tangible properties are governed through registration or business contract processes. But rights related to intangible properties is difficult to manage, as it involves the intellect of humans. (Mind)

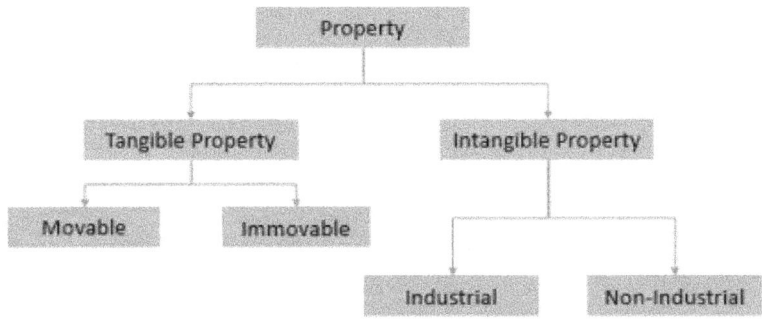

1.1 Types of Properties

Meaning and Definition of Intellectual Property

Intellectual Property is defined as any creation made possible by the application of human intelligence. It results from 2 factors:

1. Labour
2. Intellectual Capabilities.

The World Intellectual Property Organization (WIPO) defines intellectual property (IP) as works of literature, art, inventions, designs, and names, symbols, and pictures that are used in trade. Protecting creations of the mind is the main function of Intellectual property rights (IPR).

For Eg: Mr. X Invented a new battery which lasts for 10 days irrespective of the number of hours usage. This is a new invention by him against traditional batteries which will exhaust based on the use. In this case this invention should be protected and no one else should be able to use it to produce / sell other than the inventor for a specified period. Basic purpose behind this protection is to make the inventor recover his expenses of invention and make some profits. If there is no protection, then it kills the spirit of invention and all the efforts made by the inventor.

Eg. Mr. Z author of most popular book seeks copyright of his book, which makes others to not copy or reprint the contents of the book.

According to WIPO convention Article 2 (viii) Intellectual property right shall include the rights relating to:

1. Literacy, artistic and scientific work.
2. Performances of performing artists, phonograms, and broadcasts.
3. Invention in all fields of human endeavor.
4. Scientific discoveries.
5. Industrial designs.
6. Trademarks, service marks, and commercial names.
7. Protection against unfair competitions and all other rights resulting from intellectual activity in the industrial, science, literary or artistic field.

Unauthorized use of any IPR property is called an infringement and these are punishable offences.

Different Forms of IPR

IPRs encompass various forms of intangible properties that are protected. Here are different types of IPR in India:-

Patent, Trademarks, Geographical Indications, Designs, Plant varieties and Semiconductor Integrated layouts. Further Copyrights is the IPR available for non-industrial products.

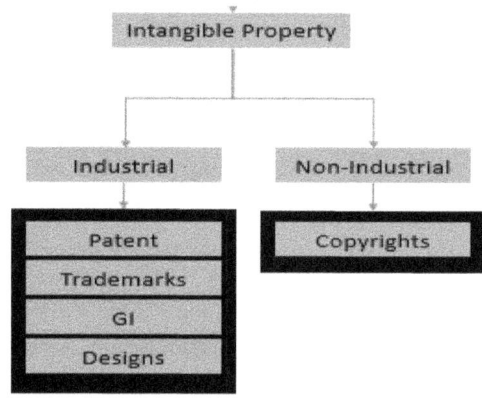

1.2 Intangible Properties and IPR

Patent: It is a statutory privilege granted by the government to inventors and to other persons deriving their rights from the inventor for fixed years to exclude other persons from manufacturing, using, or selling a patented product or processes.

Eg: New drug invented by company should not be used by other manufacturers.

E.g. Covaxin, Indian invention for the covid protection vaccine, should not produced and sold by other manufacturers for next 20 years.

Trademarks: Trademark means a mark capable of being represented graphically and which can distinguish the goods or services of one person from those of other and may include shape of goods, their packaging and combination of colours (section 2 (zb) of Trademark Act, 1999). A trademark distinguishes one company product from other company. Once registered trademarks will be valid for 10 years and can be renewed any number of times for every 10 years.

E.g. Pepsi is a trademark of Pepsi Co for its cola drink, same way Coca Cola is a registered trademark of Coca cola Inc.

Geographical Indications: these are indications which identify a goods as originating in the territory of a member, or a region or locality in that territory, where a given quality, reputation, or other characteristics of the good is attributable to geographic region. The purpose of this identification is to protect customers from buying fake Geographically indications tagged product.

Eg: Mysore Silk Sarees: This tag is associated with Karnataka Silk Industries Corporation (KSIC), and one should use this tag other than KSIC.

Designs: Design projects the form of outward appearance or aesthetic style of an object and does not protect functionality or unseen internal design elements.

Eg: Coca Cola bottle design, KitKat chocolate design etc.

Copyright: Copyright protects the expression of literary and artistic work. Protection arises automatically giving the holder the exclusive right to control reproduction or adaption of his work. Copyright owners have exclusive rights to perform, translate, adapt and license their work.

Eg: Author's right on the books written by him, Music rights of a music director etc.

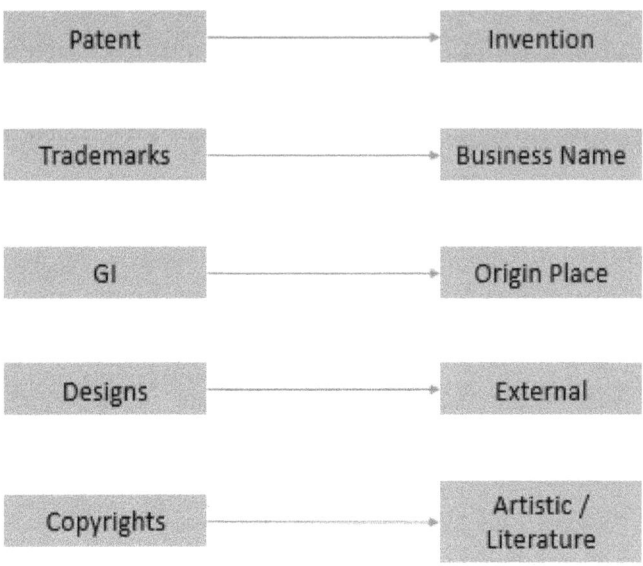

1.3 IPR and Activities

Historical Development of IPR

Intellectual property rights are not a recent origin. IPR has a long history and have played a significant role in the development of businesses over centuries. Its history can be traced back to 500 BCE when Sybaris state in Greece granted one year pat. for inventions in luxury, further, to protect the inventions and copyrights IPR was introduced in Monopolies in 1623. Post that many countries started introducing IPR related legislations.

1970: Ownership rights: Author or inventor can retain ownership for 14 years. The US also started introducing IPRs from 1800 after broke away from UK. All the states passed IPR legislations except Delaware.

Below are a few conventions:

- The Paris Convention of 1883 focuses on the Protection of Industrial Property.
- The Berne Convention of 1886 addresses the Protection of Literary and Artistic Works.
- The Brussels Convention, dealing with the Distribution of Program Carrying Signals Transmitted by Satellite.
- The Budapest Treaty of 1977 pertains to the International Recognition of the Deposit of Microorganisms for Patent Procedure.
- The 1989 Treaty on the International Registration of Audio-visual Works, also known as the Film Register Treaty.
- The Hague Agreement of 1925 concerns the International Registration of Industrial Designs.
- The Lisbon Agreement safeguards Appellations of Origin and their International Registration.
- The Locarno Agreement, established for the International Classification for Industrial Designs.
- The Madrid System, consisting of the Madrid Agreement and Madrid Protocol, governs the International Trademark System.
- The Nairobi Treaty focuses on the Protection of the Olympic Symbol.
- The 1970 Patent Cooperation Treaty (PCT) streamlines global patent procedures.
- The 1971 Convention for the Protection of Producers of Phonograms Against Unauthorized Duplication safeguards Phonograms.

- ✓ The Rome Convention pertains to the Protection of Performers, Producers of Phonograms, and Broadcasting Organizations.
- ✓ The Singapore Treaty addresses the Law of Trademark.
- ✓ The Strasbourg Agreement deals with the International Patent Classification.
- ✓ The Vienna Agreement establishes an International Classification of the Figurative Elements of Marks.
- ✓ The Washington Treaty of Intellectual Property in Respect of Integrated Circuits.
- ✓ The WIPO Copyright Treaty (WCT) governs copyright matters.
- ✓ The WIPO Performances and Phonograms Treaty addresses issues related to performances and phonograms.
- ✓ The TRIPS Agreement oversees treaties administered by WIPO in the context of international trade.

Significance of IPR in the present scenario

- ⋏ **Innovative idea a means to earn profit** - The value of ideas is often minimal on their own, but intellectual property (IP) holds significant untapped potential to transform innovations into commercially viable products and services. Registering copyright and patents can generate a consistent stream of fees and increased income, contributing to overall market success.

- ⋏ **Export Business Opportunities** - Intellectual property enhances a company's productivity in the export market. IP right holders can leverage logos or designs to market products and services internationally, establishing franchise agreements with overseas corporations or exporting proprietary products.

- ⋏ **Fostering Ideas through Security** - Individuals with unique concepts or developments may encounter attempts at unauthorized duplication for financial gain. It is crucial to safeguard intellectual property until any third party engages in unlawful infringement. IP protection can be implemented for businesses of all sizes, and the choice of Intellectual

Property Rights (trademark, copyright, or patent registration) should align with market needs and conditions.

- **Business Growth** - Safeguarding exclusive goods or services is particularly vital for small-scale enterprises, as competitors may attempt to seize market share. Protecting against such threats ensures steady growth and profits, preventing the potential danger of losing market share at the initial stages, which could negatively impact overall corporate health.

Summary

- Property is one which can be owned by an individual, corporation or any legal person and enjoy end-to-end rights related to property - sell, improve, lease, earn from the asset, or destroy the asset. These properties can be classified into - Tangible and Intangible properties.

- Intangible properties can be of Industrial and Non-Industrial. Intellectual Property Rights are related to Intangible properties. IPR deals with the intellectual aspects of the human being and assets will not physically exist.

- According to WIPO Intellectual property (IP) refers to creations of the mind, such as inventions; literary and artistic works; designs; and symbols, names and images used in commerce. Protecting creations of the mind is the main function of Intellectual property rights (IPR).

- Patents, Trademarks, Design, Geographical Indication, Copyright are the key forms of Intellectual property rights. Copyrights are related to non-industrial products whereas other forms are related to industrial products.

- The Paris convention of 1883 is the first formal convention on IPR in the world and the subject matter of the convention was protection of industrial property.

- IPR is an innovative idea to earn profit, increase export opportunities and enable business growth.

Questions

1. Examine why the protection of industrial properties is more of a necessity than a compulsion.

2. Explore the concept of intellectual property rights and delve into the historical background of the development of these rights.

3. Define intellectual property and provide a brief discussion on the various forms it takes.

4. Discuss the significance of intellectual property as a hidden yet crucial asset for accumulating tangible wealth.

5. Analyze the assertion that intellectual property is a right existing in intangible incorporeal property.

Patents

Patent

Introduction and overview of patent protection; History of patent protection; Meaning and definition of patent; Object of patent.

Patent Act

Scope and silent features of Patent Act; How to obtain a patent; Product patent and Process patent; Specification - Provisional and complete specification; Opposition proceedings to grant of patents; Register of patents and patent office; Rights and obligation of Patentee; Transfer of patent rights; Compulsory Licenses; Government use of inventions; Revocation and surrender of patents; Infringement of patents; Offences and penalties.

Case laws - Summary - Questions from Previous year question papers.

Meaning and Definition of Patent

According to Sec 2 (m)(1) of the Patent Act, Patent is defined as "a patent for any invention granted under the Act". This definition is not providing more details about what is patent.

Most widely defined definition on patent is "a statutory privilege granted by the government to inventors and to other persons deriving their rights from the inventor for fixed years to exclude other persons from manufacturing, using, or selling a patented product or processes."

Essentials of Patents

1. It is a statutory recognition by the government.
2. As it is granted by the government, it is restricted to specific countries only.
3. It is granted to Inventors for inventions.
4. It restricts other people from manufacturing, using, or selling a patented product or processes.
5. It is for the stipulated period (currently it is for 20 years).
6. Patents will be provided for both product and processes.

What is Invention?

According to sec 2 (j) of the Patent Act = Invention means a new product or process involving an inventive step and capable of Industrial application.

Essentials of Invention

1. It must be a unique product.
2. Involving Inventive Step.
3. Invention must have some economic signification.

So, Patent can be granted to only those requests where Novelty, Utility and Inventiveness exist in any innovation. These are called three tests of Patentability.

Novelty: Novelty lies in the fact that it is a new and no one has experienced it before. Inventions must not be disclosed anywhere in the world. Novelty is lost on the first sale, so before applying for patent, it is necessary to ensure that the invention is not available in the market of other countries.

Utility: The invention must have commercial utility; the invention must also be related to the field of technology (the branch of knowledge dealing with engineering or applied sciences).

Inventiveness: It is a test to determine whether the invention has significant improvement over present art, or it is just a minor improvement. Further if the delta between earlier art and the new one is significant the next step is to determine whether that delta invention requires any specific skills required or from ordinary creativity can be achieved. If it requires special skill, then qualifies for patentability.

All the above three tests to be passed for any product to get patent from the patenting authority.

Case: Novartis Case on Evergreen Patentability

Extending patent over 20 years with slightly altered or different version is not considered as invention. Getting patents renewed with small modification leads to evergreen patentability. So, invention should be significantly different than the present art.

Process Vs Product Patent

Process Patent: Under a process patent, the patent is granted for a particular manufacturing process and not for the product itself. Any other manufacturer can produce the same product but with a different process. Prior to 2005 Act, process patents were granted in respect of Food, pharma, and drug industries. Process Patent provides less protection to inventors as anyone can produce the same good with modified business process. But the advantage of process patent is it reduces the element of monopoly in the business.

Product Patent: Product Patent is granted for a specific product. Manufacturing or selling patented products is an infringement and bound by penalties. This offers higher protection for inventors and decreases competition. Major drawback of this is it promotes Monopoly, and it is not good for any economy.

TRIPS agreement proposes that every country must shift from 'Process Patent' to 'Product Patent.'

No	Basis	Product Patent	Process Patent
1	Definition	Patent protection is extended to either the 'End Result' or 'the product.'	Process patent protection is granted exclusively to the process itself and does not extend to the resultant 'End Product.'
2	Competition	Once protection is granted, less competition	Competition shall remain
3	Monopoly	The inventor experiences an elevated level of monopoly.	Inventors do not enjoy a monopoly since other people can still manufacture the same product using a different process.
4	Implementation	Product Patents were introduced as part of the Patents (Amendment) Act, 2005.	Process Patents have been recognized in India ever since the Indian Patent Act, 1970 was enforced.
5	Example	Final Product	Only process

History of Patent Protection

Word Scenario

500 BCE: Sybaris (Greek State) introduced one year patent protection for invention in luxury.

1623 - Industry Property Legislature: This British law was passed in the State of Monopolies and introduced copyright, patent, and other IPRs.

1710 - Ownership Rights: It enhanced the ownership rights of writers and inventors. Period of patent copyright extended to 14 years.

1710 - Statue of Anne: This statute allowed renewal of IPR related to copyright after 14 years.

Early 1800 - Statues in US: After breaking up from UK, United States divided into 13 states. All the states except Delaware introduced IPR laws. Later, US Federal Law was enacted on IPRs which is applicable to all the states.

1883 - Paris Convention: This is the first international convention on IPR. This was focused on Intellectual property rights for industrial products. It laid down three basic principles for granting patents worldwide - Nationality, Priority and Country specific control. Post this many conventions and treaties entered by member states.

1970 - Patent Cooperation Treaty: This was signed in Washington in 1970. With PCT patent seeker can file one application in one language within 12 months from the date of first application to get patent in multiple countries.

Indian Scenario

1911 – First Act on IPR was passed by British Government.

1970 – Indian Patent Act was passed.

1972 – Indian Patent Rules introduced.

1995 – Joined World Trade Organization (WTO).

1995 – Member of TRIPS agreement.

1998 – Became member of Paris Convention.

1998 – Joined PCT.

2005 – Patent Amendment Act passed.

The Office of the Controller General of Patents, Designs and Trademarks (CGPDT) a statutory body is responsible for administering the patent in India. Office of CGPDT is in Mumbai.

Head Quarters of Patent office is in Kolkata and has branches in New Delhi, Mumbai, and Chennai.

Object of Patent: A patent Serves Several important purposes:

1. Promotes innovation via the protection of intellectual property rights.
2. Promotes technology diffusion via publication and access to patent documents.
3. Promotes international protection of technology through international filings.
4. Promotes transfer of technology through contractual mechanism
5. Create economic value of exclusive rights.

Indian Patent Act Overview

Indian Patent Act - 1970 along with Patent Rules was introduced in 1972 by replacing existing Indian Patent and Design Act - 1911. This Act undergone a series of amendments in 1999, 2002, 2005 and 2006. Amendment of 2005 brought in major changes in the Patent Act.

Indian Patent Act has twenty-three chapters and 163 sections. Key sections covered in the books are.

- Key Definitions (Section 2).
- Application (Section 6 to 11).
- Publication and Examination of Application (Section 11A to 21).
- Grounds of Opposition (Section 25 to 28).

- Right of Patentee (Section 48).
- Exceptions to Patentee's rights / Regulatory Use / Prior Use Exemption (Section 47, 49, 100, 101, 102, 107A).
- Compulsory Licensing (Section 82 to 94).
- Surrender and Revocation (Section 63 and Section 64).
- Transfer of Patent / Assignment (Section 68 to 70).
- Suits concerning Infringement (104 to 115).
- Appeals (116 to 117).
- Penalties (118 to 124).
- Remedies and Reliefs (Section 108).
- Patent Office and Establishment (Section 73 to 76).

The 2005 amendment is a major amendment to Patent Act of 1970 which brought in following key changes.

1. Extension of product patent protection to products in sectors of drugs, foods and chemical.

2. The term for protection of product patent shall be for 20 years and are territorial rights granted by individual countries or regions.

3. Introduction of a provision for enabling grant of compulsory license for export of medicines to countries which have insufficient or no manufacturing capacity; provided such importing country has either granted a compulsory license for import or by notification or otherwise allowed importation of the patented pharmaceutical products from India (in accordance with the Doha Declaration on TRIPS and Public Health).

Key Definitions

Section 2 of the Act deals with definitions. Key definitions covered here are - Invention and Patent.

Invention

As per Section 2 (j) defined Invention means a new product or process involving an inventive step and capable of industrial application'.

Patent

A patent is granted for any invention granted under this Act to protect the rights.

Procedure for Grant of Patent

Process of Application starts with applying for patent in prescribed form by the eligible applicant. Further its passthrough Examination and Publication, once the controller satisfied with the process, then patent will be granted.

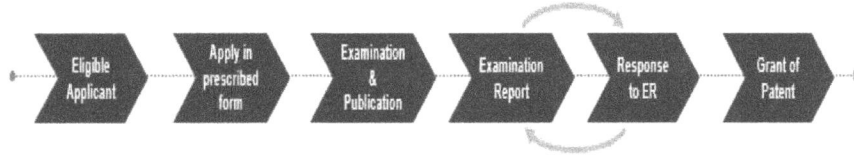

Fig 2.1: Process of Patent Application

Eligible Applicant (Sec-6)

Patent application can be submitted by

1. True and first inventor of the invention.
2. Assignee of the first inventor.
3. Legal representative of the inventor or the assignee.

Patents can be applied solely or jointly by the parties.

Any nationals can apply for patent in India.

Exception (Section 134): If Central Government by notification lists the countries where nationals of the notified countries are not eligible for applying for patent in India on the basis not providing reciprocity in that country.

Explanation:

If Indian Nationals are not allowed for licensing in Country B, then Country B nationals are not eligible for applying patent in India.

Form of Application (Sec-7)

Each patent application must pertain to a single invention, following the prescribed format, and must be submitted to the Patent office.

Application made through Patent Cooperation Treaty will be considered as an application under this Act. Original application date in first country will be considered as filing date of PCT application.

Assignee must submit proof of assignment along with the application.

Every application must state the applicant is in possession of an invention and shall the name the person claiming to be true and first inventor or authorized assignee.

Every application shall be accompanied by a provisional or complete specification.

Patent Cooperation Treaty (PCT)

Applicant after filing Patent application in one country can apply to other country through PCT. With PCT single application in single language to be submitted for registration of patent in multiple countries. PCT is administered by WIPO, this application should be submitted within 12 months from the date of first filing.

Provisional and Complete Specification (Sec-9-10)

In the overall process of securing patents, specification document is one of the critical documents. This will include a full detail about claims and disclosures related to the inventions. Patent specification is highly technical legal document which covers the details of latest available product and the subject matter of the new patent by the applicant. Grant of patent rights is depending on the content of the specification document. There are two types of specification documents.

a. Provisional Specification

b. Complete Specification

A Provisional Specification provides key information about the invention and details will be available in the complete specification. The purpose of filing provisional specification is to claim a date of priority. Provisional specification cannot be filed by the applicant in case of convention or PCT applications. A provisional specification must contain.

- Description and Title of the invention of the inventor.
- It is recommended to exclude any of the claims.
- Main Objects of the invention include the background of the invention and the statement of the invention.

When submitting a patent application, a provisional specification is allowed initially, but within 12 months, the patent applicant must submit a complete specification; failure to do so will result in the application being deemed abandoned.

A complete specification is a comprehensive document providing detailed information about the invention, encompassing the full design, solution, claims, and disclosures. It is mandatory for all applications related to PCT and other conventions and treaties for the national phase. The crucial components of a complete specification include:

- ✓ A thorough and explicit description of the invention, its operation or use, and the method by which it is to be performed.
- ✓ Disclosure of the best method of performing the invention known to the applicant, for which protection is sought.
- ✓ Ending with one or more claims that define the scope of the invention for which protection is claimed.

Additionally:

- ✓ An abstract is required to offer technical information on the invention, with the provision for the Controller to amend it for better clarity.
- ✓ If a biological material is mentioned, not adequately described to satisfy certain conditions, and is not available to the public, the

applicant must deposit it with an international depository authority under the Budapest Treaty. Specific conditions, including disclosure details, must be fulfilled.

✓ For international applications designating India, the filed title, description, drawings, abstract, and claims are considered the complete specification.

✓ The claims of a complete specification should pertain to a single invention or a group of inventions forming a single inventive concept. They must be clear, concise, and fairly based on the disclosed matter.

Examination and Publication (Sec-11A-21)

Publication of applications (Section 11A)

In accordance with intellectual property rights (IPR), once the patent office receives a patent application, it is typically not disclosed to the public for a duration specified by regulations. Following this prescribed period, the Controller is responsible for promptly publishing the application, unless certain conditions warrant a delay. Publication may be deferred by the Controller under the following circumstances:

- A secrecy direction is imposed under Section 35.
- The application has been abandoned under Sub-section (1) of Section 9.
- The application has been withdrawn three months prior to the period specified in Section 11A (1).
- In the case of a secrecy directive, publication may occur after the specified period has elapsed or when the secrecy direction ceases to operate, whichever is later.

Content of the Publication:
- Date of application.
- Number of applications.
- Name and address of the applicant.
- An abstract.

From the date of publication until the patent is granted, the applicant is entitled to similar privileges and rights as if the patent had been granted on the publication date. However, the applicant cannot initiate infringement proceedings until the patent is officially granted.

Request for Examination (Sec-11B):

No examination of a patent application takes place unless the applicant or another interested party submits a request in the prescribed manner within the specified timeframe. Failure to request examination within this period may result in the application being treated as withdrawn, except under certain circumstances:

1. The applicant can withdraw the application at any time after filing but before the patent is granted by making a request in the prescribed manner.
2. In cases where a secrecy direction has been issued under Section 35, the request for examination may be made within the prescribed period from the date of revocation of the secrecy direction.

Once the Controller receives the examination request, it is forwarded to an examiner, who assesses:

- Compliance with the Act and relevant rules.
- The presence of any lawful grounds for objection to the patent grant.
- The results of investigations made under Section 13.
- Any other matter as prescribed.

The examiner submits a report to the Controller within the prescribed period, conducting a detailed inquiry into existing patents in the related field.

The Controller may accept the report and proceed with the acceptance of the application, refuse it, or request amended applications. In cases of applications covering multiple inventions, the Controller may instruct the division of the application into two or more separate applications.

The Controller is empowered to determine the patent grant date following a review and recommendations, with the stipulation that no application can be post-dated under this provision to a date beyond six months from its original submission.

In situations involving potential infringement, the Controller possesses the authority to instigate an inquiry and request evidence.

Upon receiving a request from the patentee, the Controller holds the authority to substitute ownership.

Grounds of Opposition (Sec-25-28)

An affected party holds the right to oppose a patent either before its grant, known as Pre-Grant Opposition, or after its grant, referred to as Post-Grant Opposition. Pre-grant opposition can be raised within six months from the date of publication, while post-grant opposition can be initiated within 12 months from the date of the patent grant's publication in the official Journal of the patent office.

The grounds for opposition include:

1. Obtaining the patent through wrongful means.
2. Publication of the invention prior to the patent application.
3. The invention was publicly known or used in India before the priority date of that claim.
4. The invention is apparent and lacks any innovative step.
5. The subject of any claim is not deemed an invention within the meaning of the Act or is not eligible for patent protection under this act.
6. Inadequate disclosure of the invention or the method by which it is to be executed.
7. In the case of a patent granted based on a convention application, the patent application was not submitted within 12 months from the date of the initial application for protection for the invention made in a convention country or in India.

8. The complete specification fails to reveal or inaccurately states the source and geographical origin of biological material used for the invention.

9. The invention was expected, considering the knowledge, oral, or otherwise available within any local or Indigenous community in India or elsewhere.

What are not Inventions (Sec-3)

As per Section-3 of the act, the following are not considered as inventions:

1. Any invention deemed frivolous or making claims obviously contrary to well-established national laws.

2. An invention, the primary or intended use or commercial exploitation of which would contravene public order or morality, or cause serious harm to human, animal, plant life, health, or the environment.

3. The mere discovery of scientific principles or the formulation or discovery of any living or non-living substance occurring in nature.

4. The mere discovery of a new form of a known substance does not result in enhanced known efficacy.

5. A substance obtained by mere admixture resulting only in the aggregation of the properties of its components or a process for producing such a substance.

6. The mere arrangement, rearrangement, or duplication of known devices, each functionally independent of one another in a known way.

7. A method of agriculture or horticulture.

8. Any process for the medicinal, surgical, prophylactic, or other treatment of human beings or any other processes.

9. Plants and animals in whole or any part thereof, excluding microorganisms but including seeds, varieties, species, and biological processes for the production or propagation of plants and animals.
10. A mathematical or business method or a computer program per se or algorithm.
11. A literary, dramatic, musical, or artistic work, or any other aesthetic creation, including cinematographic works and television production.
12. A mere scheme or rule or method of performing a mental act or method of playing games.
13. The presentation of information.
14. Topography of integrated circuits.
15. An invention which, in effect, is traditional knowledge or a known component.

Compulsory Licensing (Sec-82)

Sometimes for the benefit of the publicGovernment may grant permission to produce patented product to other parties without the permission of the patentee. This kind of grant is called as Compulsory Licensing. Section 82 to 94 (Chapter - XVI) of Indian Patent Act deals with the compulsory licensing. Government grants compulsory licensing only if the below conditions are satisfied.

1. This can be granted only after the expiration of 3 years from the grant of patent.
2. A person interested in using the patent must request for the grant of patent. Subject to following condition (Section -84).
3. The public's reasonable requirements concerning the patented innovation have not been fulfilled.
4. The patented invention is not accessible to the public at a reasonable price.

5. The patented invention is not put into operation within the territory of India.

This is commonly referred to as "Abuse of Patents," serving as an exception to the rights of the patentee outlined in Section 48 of the Act.

In seeking the grant of a patent, the applicant must meet the above conditions. Additionally, the applicant must have attempted to secure a license from the patentee under reasonable terms and conditions. If these efforts prove unsuccessful within a period deemed reasonable by the controller, the applicant can proceed with the application.

- In Aug 2011, Natco applied for compulsory licensing for anti-cancer drug Nexavar.
- Patent for the said drug was owned by Bayer's Pharmaceuticals, US
- Indian Patent office granted the compulsory license to Natco pharma on the ground that all the three grounds mentioned in section-84.
    - Only 2% of the patient population was using this in India – Reasonable requirements not met.
    - It was priced at Rs.2,80,000 against Natco Pharma was willing to supply at Rs.8800 – Reasonably not priced
    - Bayer's did not manufacture this drug in India.
- Natco pharma got compulsory licensing rights on the terms that the payment of a royalty pegged at 6% of quarterly royalty of net sales, payable to Bayer's.
- Bayer's took this to appeal at Intellectual Property Appellate Board (IPAB)
- IPAB considering the facts, and on finding that the insufficient numbers and the prohibitively expensive product, held that Bayer was not satisfying the reasonable requirements of the public for the drug.
    - Declared compulsory licensing grant is valid.
    - Bayer's can avoid this grant by selling products at lower prices.
    - Royalty payable was increased from 6% to 7%.

The landmark case in India is the Bayer's Vs Natco Pharma case where compulsory licensing granted to Natco Pharma to produce Nexavar drug which was owned by Bayer's.

Surrender is a voluntary forgoing the patent right by submitting application to Patent office. On the other hand, Revocation is involuntary withdrawal of patent by the Patent office on the grounds of ineligibility or other reasons specified in Section-64.

Surrender and Revocation of Patent (Sec-63-64)

Surrender of Patent (Section-63)

A patentee may offer to surrender his / her patent at any time by giving notice to the controller. Post review of the document, controller will publish the offer and notify every person whose name appears in the register.

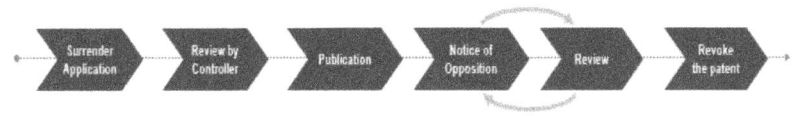

2.2 Surrender of Patent

Interested person may give notice of opposition to surrender of patent to controller. The review process continues and once reaching to a conclusion between opposite party and patentee, the controller accepts the surrender request and will revoke the patent.

Revocation of Patent (Section-64)

Revocation of patent can be initiated by Patent office on the following grounds if the application is submitted by concerned or aggrieved party.

    a. **Duplicate:** Complete specification submitted by patent applicant is same as other patent application submitted before the priority date.

    b. **Qualification:** That the patent granted on the application of a person not entitled under the provision of this Act to apply.

c. **Contravention of Rights:** If the patent was obtained wrongfully in contravention of the rights of the petitioner or any person under or through whom he claims.

d. **Not and Invention:** If the subject of the claim is not an invention within the meaning of this Act.

e. **Publicly Known**: If the content of complete specification was known to public before priority date.

f. **No Inventive Step:** Lack of Inventive Step: The invention, as claimed in any of the complete specification's claims, is not novel, considering what was publicly known or used in India before the claim's priority date or what was published in India or elsewhere in any of the documents mentioned in Section 13.

g. **Not Useful**: If the invention is not useful in any manner to people or society.

h. **Obvious**: If the invention does not contain any inventive step in comparison to existing

i. **No Clarity:** that the scope of any claim of the complete specification is not sufficiently and clearly defined or that any claim of the complete specification is not fairly based on the matter disclosed in the specification.

j. **False representation:** that the patent was obtained on a false suggestion or representation.

k. **Subject Matter:** That the subject of any claim of the complete specification is not patentable under this Act.

l. **Secret usage:** that the invention as far as claimed in any claim of the complete specification was secretly used in India, otherwise than as mentioned in sub-section (3), before the priority date of the claim.

m. **Partial Information:** that the applicant for the patent has failed to disclose to the Controller the information required by section 8 or has furnished information which in any material was false to his knowledge.

n. **Directions:** that the applicant contravened any direction for secrecy passed under section 35.

o. **Fraud:** that leave to amend the complete specification under section 57 or section 58 was obtained by fraud.

Importing of Patent

If the applicant is an importer of patent, on this ground revocation cannot be done. While considering the imported patent used in India following points to be considered.

a. No account shall be taken of secret use; and

b. Where the patent is for a process or for a product as made by a process described or claimed, the importation into India of the product made abroad by that process shall constitute knowledge or use in India of the invention on the date of the importation, except where such importation has been for the purpose of reasonable trial or experiment only.

Revocation by High Court

In addition to the provisions in subsection (1), the High Court, upon the petition of the Central Government, may revoke a patent if it is convinced that the patentee, without reasonable cause, has not complied with the Central Government's request to utilize the patented invention for governmental purposes as defined in section 99, subject to reasonable terms.

Revocation Procedure

A notification of any petition seeking the revocation of a patent under this section must be delivered to all individuals identified in the register as patent proprietors or as having shares or interests in the patent. Serving notice to any other person is not required.

Intellectual Property Rights-1

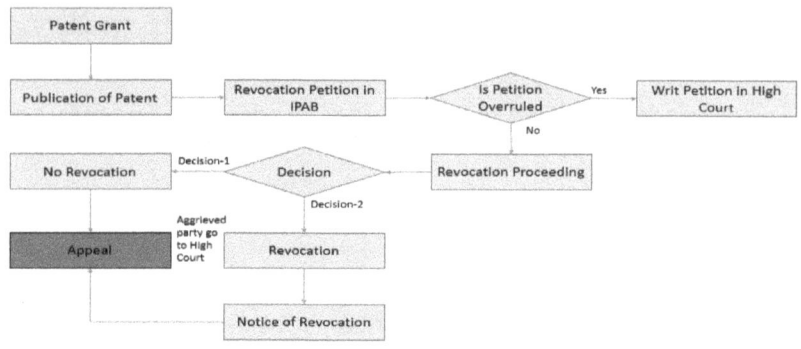

2.3 Revocation of Patent

Rights of Patentee (Sec-48) and Exceptions

Every Patent holder will have exclusive right to prevent third parties use of patent without patentee's consent. Exclusive Use includes - making, using, offering for sale, selling, or importing.

Exceptions

1. **Section-47:** Grant of Patent to be subject to certain conditions:

    i. Government can import / make any patented invention for its own use or authorize someone to import or manufacture.

    ii. The government can use any patented process for its own use.

    iii. Experimental or Scientific use including imparting of instruction to pupil.

    iv. Government may import any patented medicine or drug for its own use or for distribution in Govt. establishment.

2. **Section 107:** A-Bolar Provision

    Any act of making, constructing using, selling or importing a patented invention solely for uses reasonably related to the development and submission of information required under any law for the time being in force, in India, or in a country other than India, the regulates the

Intellectual Property Rights - 1

manufacture, construction, use, sale or import of any product does not amount to an infringement of patent right of the patent owner.

> **Bolar Provision**
>
> The Bolar provision allows the generic producers to market and manufacture their goods as soon as the patent term expires, but does not allow for the use of patented drug to distribute the generic drug before the expiry of the term of patent.

3. **Section 100-102:** Rights of third parties in respect of use of invention for the purpose of Government:

   a. **Section 100:** Central Government and any person authorized in writing by it, may use the invention for the purposes of Government in accordance with the provisions of this Chapter. The patentee must allow any use of the invention by the Central Government, or any person authorized in writing by it for the purposes of Government may be made free of any royalty or other remuneration to the patentee.

   b. **Section 102:** The Central Government may, if satisfied that it is necessary that an invention which is the subject of an application for a patent or a patent should be acquired from the applicant or the patentee for a public purpose, publish a notification to that effect in the Official Gazette, and thereupon the invention or patent and all rights in respect of the invention or patent shall, by force of this section, stand transferred to and be vested in the Central Government. Notice of the acquisition shall be given to the applicant, and, where a patent has been granted, to the patentee and other persons, if any, appearing in the register as having an interest in the patent.

4. **Section-49:** Patent right no infringed when used on foreign vessel temporarily or accidently in India: Where a vessel or aircraft registered in a foreign country or a land vehicle owned by a person ordinarily resident in such country comes into India (including the territorial

waters thereof) temporarily or accidentally only, the rights conferred by a patent for an invention shall not be deemed to be infringed by the use of the invention -

a. In the body of the vessel or in the machinery, tackle, apparatus, or other accessories thereof, as far as the invention is used on board the vessel and for its actual needs only; or

b. In the construction or working of the aircraft or land vehicle or of the accessories thereof.

Transfer of Patent (Sec-68-69)

A patentee is an absolute owner of the patent and without his permission no one can use the patented product and services (Section-48). On the other hand, few conditions and exceptions are provided in Section 47, 49, 100, 101, 102 and 107A for the use of patented product or service without Patentee's approval. Apart from the above, using patented product or services is infringement. But patentee may officially transfer the right to use to other party.

Transfer of patents can happen through any one of the following modes.

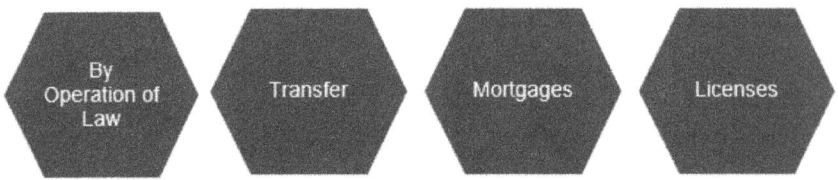

2.4 Transfer of Patent

5. **By operation law:** It is a natural transmission of patent to legal heirs of the deceased patent holder. In case of a death of patent holder the patent property will be transferred to legal heir of the patent holder or as per the will of the patent holder. Updating of Patent register is a must in this case.

6. **Transfer of patent:** Here patent holder voluntarily transfers full or partial rights to patent holder through some deed or agreement. The patent holder gets a right in this only if the deed is registered and details of the ownership are entered in the patent registrar at Patent office.

7. **Mortgage:** Patentee can mortgage patent with others for the purpose of getting money or any other reasons. Once the agreed amount is returned to Mortgagor, Patentee will get back the rights of patent. This transaction does not require any updating in Patent Registrar.

8. **License:** Patent licensing agreements are contracts in which the patent owner (the licensor) agrees to grant the licensee the right to make, use, sell, and/or import the claimed invention, usually in return for royalty or other compensation.

The transfer of a patent or any portion thereof, whether through assignment, mortgage, license, or the establishment of any other interest in a patent, shall only be considered legally binding if documented in writing. The agreement between the involved parties must be formalized into a document that comprehensively captures all terms and conditions dictating their rights and responsibilities, and this document must be duly executed by the parties involved.

Registration of assignment

1. Where any person becomes entitled by way of assignment stated above, he shall apply in writing in the prescribed manner to the Controller for the registration of his title or of notice of his interest in the register.

2. In certain cases, assignor, mortgagor, licensor may also make an application to patent office for registration.

3. If there is any confusion, conflict or dispute exist in the title, then registrar can refuse to register the assignment. Once the rights of the parties have been determined by a competent court then the Registrar can proceed with the registration.

Except as stipulated in this Act concerning co-ownership of patents and taking into account any rights officially recorded in the register under the name of another person, the individual or individuals officially listed as the grantee or owner of a patent shall possess the authority to transfer, issue licenses for, or engage in any other transactions involving the patent. They are also empowered to issue valid receipts for any consideration received in connection with such assignments, licenses, or transactions. It is noteworthy that any legal claims related to the patent's ownership may be pursued in a manner similar to that of any other movable property.

Infringement, Relief & Remedies, Penalties and Appeal

In this part, the following points are discussed.

- ⮞ Suits concerning Infringement (Sec-104 to Sec-115).
- ⮞ Appeals (Sec-116 to Sec-117).
- ⮞ Penalties (Sec-118 to Sec-124).

Suits Concerning Infringement (Sec-104 to Sec-115)

Legal actions for patent infringement cannot be initiated in any court below a district court with the appropriate jurisdiction to adjudicate the case. However, a lawsuit for a declaration can be initiated under this section at any point subsequent to the public announcement of the patent grant.

In cases of patent infringement lawsuits, the onus of proof primarily rests on the defendant. Particularly, in instances where the patent pertains to a process for producing a certain product, the court holds the authority to instruct the defendant to demonstrate that the process employed by them to create the identical product derived from the patented process is distinct from the patented process itself.

Infringement of Patents

There is no explanation or definition given in the Act about what constitutes Infringement of Patents. General meaning if any unauthorized person exercise rights and powers granted under the act to a patent holder constitutes Infringement. The following amounts to an act of patent infringement.

1. The colorable imitation of the invention.
2. Mechanical equivalent which means user of substitutes for some features, to obtain same results for the same use as done by the patentee.
3. Carrying essential features of the invention.
4. Immaterial variation in the invention.

When an individual, regardless of their entitlement or interest in a patent or patent application, issues threats of patent infringement through circulars, advertisements, or communications-whether oral or written-to another person or any party, any person adversely affected by such actions has the right to file a lawsuit seeking the following remedies:

1. A declaration affirming that the threats are unwarranted,
2. An injunction to prohibit the continuation of the threats, and
3. Damages, if incurred, because of the threats.
4. Certain acts are excluded from being deemed as infringement under this Act. These include:
5. Engaging in the acts of making, constructing, using, selling, or importing a patented invention solely for purposes reasonably linked to the development and submission of information required by prevailing laws, either in India or another country, regulating the manufacture, construction, use, sale, or import of any product.
6. The importation of patented products by an individual from an entity duly authorized by law to produce, sell, or distribute the product shall not be considered an infringement of patent rights.

Relief in suits for infringement

The reliefs which a court may grant in any suit for infringement are.

1. Injunction
2. Damages
3. Account of profit
4. Seizure, forfeit or destroy the goods.

In a patent infringement lawsuit, damages or an account of profits will not be awarded against the defendant if they can demonstrate that, at the time of the infringement, they were unaware and had no reasonable grounds to believe that the patent existed.

Appeals (Sec-116 to Sec-117)

Subject to the provisions of this Act, the Appellate Board established under section 83 of the Trademarks Act, 1999 shall be the Appellate Board for the purposes of this Act and the said Appellate Board shall exercise the jurisdiction, power and authority conferred on it by or under this Act.

Qualification of Technical member of Appellate Board

a. Has, at least five years held the post of Controller under this Act or has exercised the functions of the Controller under this Act for at least five years; or

b. Has, for at least ten years functioned as a Registered Patent Agent and possesses a degree in engineering or technology or a master's degree in science from any University established under law for the time being in force or equivalent;

Staff of Appellate Board

1. The Central Government shall determine the nature and categories of the officers and other employees required to assist the Appellate Board in the discharge of its functions under this Act and provide the Appellate Board with such officers and other employees as it may think fit.

2. The salaries and allowances and conditions of service of the officers and other employees of the Appellate Board shall be as may be prescribed.

3. The officers and other employees of the Appellate Board shall discharge their functions under the general superintendent of the Chairperson of the Appellate Board in the manner as may be prescribed.

Every appeal shall be made within three months from the date of the decision, order, or direction of the Controller or the Central Government or within such further time as the Appellate Board may, in accordance with the rules made by it allow.

Every appeal under this section shall be in the prescribed form and shall be verified in such a manner as may be prescribed and shall be accompanied by a copy of the decision, order or direction appealed against and by such fees as may be prescribed.

Penalties (Sec-118 to Sec-124)

Infringement	Penalty
Contravention of secrecy provisions relating to certain inventions	Imprisonment for a' term which may extend to two years, or with fine, or with both.
Falsification of entries in register, etc.	Punishable with imprisonment for a term which may extend to two years, or with fine, or with both.
Unauthorized claim of patent rights	Punishable with fine which may extend to one lakh rupees
Wrongful use of words "patent office"	Punishable with imprisonment for a term which may extend to six months, or with fine, or with both.
Refusal or failure to supply information to Central Government / Controller	Punishable with fine which may extend to ten lakh rupees

Practice by non-registered patent agents.	Punishable with fine which may extend to one lakh rupees in the case of a first offence and five lakh rupees in the case of a second or subsequent offence
Offences by Companies	If the person committing an offence under this Act is a company, the company as well as every person in charge of, and responsible to, the company for the conduct of its business at the time of the commission of the offence shall be deemed to be guilty of the offence and shall be liable to be proceeded against and punished accordingly

Patent Office and Establishment

The Controller General of Patents, Designs and Trademarks appointed under sub-section (1) of section 3 of the Trademarks Act, 1999 (47 of 1999), shall be the Controller of Patents for the purposes of this Act. For the purposes of this Act, the Central Government may appoint as many examiners and other officers and with such designations as it thinks fit.

For the purposes of this Act, there shall be an office which shall be known as the patent office. The Central Government may, by notification in the Official Gazette, specify the name of the Patent Office. The head office of the patent office shall be at such place as the Central Government may specify, and for the purpose of facilitating the registration of patents there may be established, at such other places as the Central Government may think fit, branch offices of the patent office. There shall be a seal of the patent office.

> **Patent Offices in India**
>
> The Office of the Controller General of Patents, Designs & Trademarks (CGPDTM) is located at Mumbai. The Head Office of the Patent office is at Kolkata and its Branch offices are located at Chennai, New Delhi, and Mumbai. The Trademarks registry is at Mumbai and its Branches are in Kolkata, Chennai, Ahmedabad, and New Delhi. The Design Office is located at Kolkata in the Patent Office. The Offices of The Patent Information System (PIS) and National Institute of Intellectual Property Management (NIIPM) are at Nagpur.

Powers of Controller General (Section-77)

The following are the key powers of Controller.

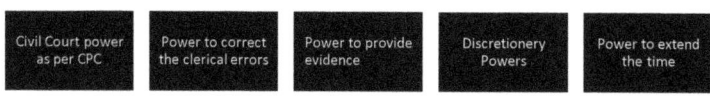

2.5: Powers of Controller General

1. Civil Court powers as per CPC

Subject to any rules made in this behalf, the Controller in any proceedings before him under this Act shall have the powers of a civil court while trying a suit under the Code of Civil Procedure, 1908 (5 of 1908), in respect of the following matters, namely: -

- a. Summoning and enforcing the attendance of any person and examining him on oath,
- b. Requiring the discovery and production of any document,
- c. Receiving evidence on affidavits 2,
- d. Issuing commissions for the examination of witnesses or documents,
- e. Awarding costs,

f. Reviewing his own decision on application made within the prescribed time and in the prescribed manner,

g. Setting aside an order passed ex-parte on application made within the prescribed time and in the prescribed manner,

h. Any other matter which may be prescribed.

Any order for costs awarded by the Controller in exercise of the powers conferred upon him as stated above shall be executable as a decree of a civil court.

2. Power to correct clerical errors

Controller may, in accordance with the provisions of this section, correct any clerical error in any patent or in any specification or other document filed in pursuance of such application or in any application for a patent or any clerical error in any matter which is entered in the register. A correction may be made in pursuance of this section either upon a request in writing made by any person interested and accompanied by the prescribed fee, or without such a request.

Where the Controller proposes to make any such correction as aforesaid otherwise than in pursuance of a request made under this section, he shall give notice of the proposal to the patentee or the applicant for the patent, as the case may be, and to any other person who appears to him to be concerned, and shall give them an opportunity to be heard before making the correction

3. Power to provide evidence

Subject to any rules made in this behalf, in any proceeding under this Act before the Controller, evidence shall be given by affidavit in the absence of directions by the Controller to the contrary, but in any case in which the Controller thinks it right so to do, he may take oral evidence in lieu of, or in addition to, evidence by affidavit, or may allow any party to be cross-examined on the contents of his affidavit.

4. Exercise of discretionary power

Without prejudice to any provision contained in this Act requiring the Controller to hear any party to the proceedings thereunder or to give any such party an opportunity to be heard, the Controller shall give to any applicant for a patent, or for amendment of a specification (if within the prescribed time the applicant so requires) an opportunity to be heard before exercising adversely to the applicant any discretion vested in the Controller by or under this Act.

5. Power to extend the time

Where under the provisions of this Act or the rules made thereunder the Controller may extend the time for doing any act, nothing in this Act shall be deemed to require him to give notice to or hear the party interested in opposing the extension, nor shall any appeal lie from any order of the Controller granting such extension.

Key Case Laws related to Patent

1. Bajaj Auto Ltd Vs TVS Motor Company Ltd

Plaintiff: Bajaj Auto Ltd.

Defendant: TVS Motor Company Limited.

Subject Matter: The case involved the unauthorized application and use of the patented Digital Twin Spark Ignition (DTSi) technology by TVS Motor Company.

Issue: Whether defendant had violated the law and applied patented innovation in an unauthorised way. Bajaj claimed that DTSi technology is an invention and falls under the ambit of 'an inventive step'. Whereas TVS claimed that the technology used in this case was prior art and it was used by US Honda for long time and argued that patent should not have granted to Bajaj.

Decision (High Court): The High Court granted temporary injunction in favour of plaintiff and instructed defendant to not to accept any order and later Injunction was vacated after the plea from the defendant.

Appeal in Supreme Court: Plaintiff appealed in supreme court, but Supreme court dismissed the appeal and stated that the Patent issues should be addressed in Trial court within stipulated time. Further, SC instructed Madras High Court to hear the case daily and close within stipulated time (30th November 2009).

Final Judgement: The matter was settled outside court after withdrawing the several pending suits from various courts and fora. The two companies entered into a settlement agreement and put the dispute to rest.

2. Bayer Corporation Vs Union of India

Plaintiff: Bayer Corporation

Defendant: Union of India

Subject Matter: Bayer corporation was the patentee of drug "Sorafenib Tosylate" which has been used to treat liver and kidney cancer since 2008. Drug controller of India granted the compulsory license to Natco Pharma for producing the generic drug. It is a first ever instance of compulsory license in India.

Fact: Bayer was selling drug at Rs. 2,80,000 per month whereas Natco promises to make it for Rs. 8800 per month.

Issue: Whether Patent issued by Drug Controller of India amounts to infringement under patent act.

Decision: High court upheld the decision of Drug Controller of India as public interest is always a priority over patent. It further stated that the acceptance of the generic drug would not amount to infringement.

3. Novartis Vs Cipla

Plaintiff: Novartis

Defendant: Cipla

Subject Matter: Novartis (Plaintiff) sued Cipla (Defendant) for infringing patents covering **Onbrez** which is an Indacaterol-drug used to treat chronic obstructive pulmonary disease and sought damages.

Facts: The drug was patent protected for both product and process patents for the last 5 years and owned by Novartis. Cipla produced the generic drug stating inadequate supply of drug as the drug used to be imported and disease was spreading like epidemic. So, defendant claimed that in the interest of public, it produced the generic drug.

Issue: Whether the production of generic drug in the public interest is infringement or not.

Decision: Delhi High Court granted the temporary injunction and barred defendant from making the generic drug. In 2017 Cipla filed the appeal and the appeal was also dismissed on the same grounds.

Summary

A patent is a statutory privilege granted by the government to inventors and to other persons deriving their rights from the inventor for fixed years to exclude other persons from manufacturing, using, or selling a patented product or processes.

- A new product, inventive step and economic significance are the three key elements of patentability of a product.

- Patents can be a process patent or product patent. The world is moving towards product patents.

- In India, first IPR act was passed in 1911 by British government. Post-Independence, 1970 Indian Patent Act is the first act in the field of IPR.

- Patents help in promoting innovation, technology diffusion, international protection, and create economic value.

- In India, Patent Act was introduced in 1970 and it was amended in 2005, where scope of the patent products increased and added drugs, foods, and chemical products. Further, the protection period of the patent was set to 20 years. Compulsory licensing was introduced in the 2005 amendment.

- Invention means a new product or process involving an inventive step and capable of industrial application.

- Process of Application starts with applying for patent in prescribed form by the eligible applicant. Further its passthrough Examination and Publication, once the controller satisfied with the process, then patent will be granted.

- Every application for a patent shall be for one invention only and shall be made in the prescribed form and filed in the Patent office.

- With Patent Cooperative Treaty, single application in single language to be submitted for registration of patent in multiple countries. PCT is administered by WIPO, this application should be submitted within 12 months from the date of first filing.

- Grant of patent rights is depending on the content of the specification document. There are two types of specification documents - Provisional Specification and Complete Specification.

- Affected party may raise opposition before granting of patent (Pre-Grant Opposition) or after granting of patent (Post grant opposition). Pre-grant opposition can be raised within six months from the date of publication whereas Post grant opposition can be raised within 12 months from the date of publication of the grant of patent in the official Journal of the patent office.

- What inventions are not defined in section-3 of the Act?

- Sometimes for the benefit of the public, the public Government may grant permission to produce patented products to other parties without the permission of the patentee. This kind of grant is called Compulsory Licensing.

- A patentee may offer to surrender his / her patent at any time by giving notice to the controller.

- Revocation of patent can be initiated by Patent office on the following grounds if concerned or aggrieved party submits the application.

- Every Patent holder will have exclusive right to prevent third parties use of patent without patentee's consent. Exclusive Use includes – making, using, offering for sale, selling, or importing.

- Exceptions to patent holder rights are covered in section-47, 107A, 100, 102 and 49.

- Assignment of patents can be affected by operation of law, transfer, mortgages, and licenses.

- General meaning if any unauthorized person exercise rights and powers granted under the act to a patent holder constitutes Infringement.

- The reliefs which a court may grant in any suit for infringement are Injunction, Damages, Account of profit and/or, Seizure, forfeit or destroy the goods.

- Subject to the provisions of this Act, the Appellate Board established under section 83 of the Trademarks Act, 1999 shall be the Appellate Board for the purposes of this Act and the said Appellate Board shall exercise the jurisdiction, power and authority conferred on it by or under this Act.

- The Office of the Controller General of Patents, Designs & Trademarks (CGPDTM) is located at Mumbai. The Head Office of the Patent office is at Kolkata and its Branch offices are located at Chennai, New Delhi, and Mumbai. The Trademarks registry is at Mumbai and its Branches are in Kolkata, Chennai, Ahmedabad, and New Delhi. The Design Office is located at Kolkata in the Patent Office. The Offices of The Patent Information System (PIS) and National Institute of Intellectual Property Management (NIIPM) are at Nagpur.

Questions

1. What is a patent? Explain legal requisites for patenting.'
2. Define Patent agent.
3. Examine the importance and types of specification under the patent law.
4. Write a note on the rights of a patentee.
5. 'X' has an invention relating to atomic energy and wants to obtain a patent for it. Advise him.
6. What are the factors responsible for the growth of patent law? Explain.
7. Write a brief note on surrender and revocation of patent.

8. Discuss special provisions for compulsory licenses under sections 92 and 92 A of the Patents Act, 1970.

9. Concise note on Meaning Of "Inventive Step."

10. Give an overview of law of grant of patents in India. Explain the meaning of 'invention, inventive step, and concept of evergreening. Also, state whether the method of curing a disease in humans or animals is patentable.

11. Write a concise note on Evergreening of patent.

12. Define Patent and what are the rights of patentee?

13. Define an "Invention." Describe the yardsticks that determine the patentability of an invention.

14. Discuss the various rights available to a patentee. Examine the limitations imposable on Patentee's right.

15. Who can file an application for a patent? Discuss the procedure for acceptance of application and grant of patent.

16. What is infringement and discuss the various legal relief against the infringement of patent?

17. Explain the inventions that are not patentable.

18. State the kinds of specification. Explain its contents.

Chapter 3

Trademark

Trademarks
Introduction and overview of Trademark; Evolution of Trademark Law; Meaning and Definition; Object of Trademark; Features of good Trademark; Different forms of trademark.

Trademarks Act
Trademark registry and register of trademarks; Property in trademark; Registerable and non-registerable trademarks; Basic principles of registration of trademarks; Deceptive similarity; Assignment and transmission; Rectification of register; Infringement of trademarks; Passing off; Offenses and Penalties.

Domain Names
Domain Name Protection and Registration.

Summary - Case law chart - Previous year question papers.

Introduction

A trademark encompasses any signs, symbols, designs, expressions, taglines, logos, combination of colours or abbreviations that recognize or identify a product. In India, trademarks are protected under the Trademarks Act of 1999. Trademarks are intellectual property represented as visual symbols, labels, signs, or designs that signify a manufacturer's products. They play a crucial role in helping customers distinguish one company's products or services from others. A trademark owner can be any legal entity, such as an individual, company, partnership, or another group of people.

A trademark is more than just a symbol, name, or logo; it represents trust, quality, and identity. In today's competitive business world, where countless products and services vie for customer attention, a trademark serves as a powerful tool, guiding consumers towards familiar and reliable choices. It serves as the signature of a brand, a stamp of authenticity, and a shield against imitation. Therefore, a trademark is not merely a symbol etched in ink or pixels; it is a legal construct, an asset, and a defence against infringement. Understanding the intricacies of trademark law and its implications for businesses is crucial in today's competitive marketplace.

The Trademarks Act of 1999 provides, among other things, for the registration of service marks and collective marks, enhanced protection for marks classified as reputable, and the establishment of an Intellectual Property Trial Board (IPAB) through the Amendment Act of 2010. The Trademarks (Amendment) Act of 2010 incorporated Chapter 6 into the Act, containing special provisions regarding the protection of marks through international registration under the Madrid Protocol. Thus, Indian Trademark Law covers both domestic and international trademark registration within its scope.

This introductory note sets the stage for a journey into the world of trademarks, exploring their significance, the legal framework that protects them, and the strategic importance they hold in the realm of branding and commerce.

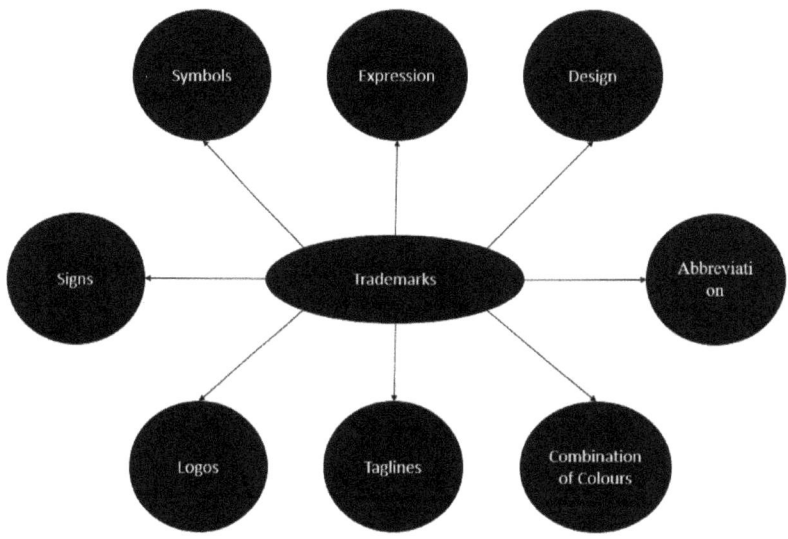

3.1: Trademarks

Evolution of Trademarks Law in India

The origins of trademark law in India can be traced back to before 1940, as there was no statutory law governing trademarks in the country at that time. Common law principles regarding trademark protection came into effect during this period. The Trademarks Act of 1940 was first enacted in India to address the absence of specific laws dealing with the intricacies of trademark infringement and communication.

India embarked on a journey to establish trademark registration and legal protection within its borders. Initially, the statutory provisions of trademark law closely mirrored English law and precedents. However, as trade and commerce expanded, the legislature recognized the need for more robust intellectual property laws, prompting revisions to existing regulations. Consequently, the Trademarks Act of 1940 was superseded by the Trademarks and Goods Trademarks Act of 1958, which also introduced the Trademarks and Goods Trademarks Regulations of 1959. The 1958 Act and its accompanying regulations aimed to strengthen trademark protection and incorporated provisions related to trademarks from other laws such as the Indian Criminal Code, Code of Criminal Procedure, and Maritime Customs Code to meet trade requirements.

In response to the evolving landscape of intellectual property rights, including adherence to Trade-Related Aspects of Intellectual Property Rights (TRIPS), and the increasing globalization of trade and technology, the Trademarks Act of 1999 and the Trademarks Rules of 2002 were formulated and came into effect on September 15, 2003.

The need for a comprehensive law exclusively addressing trademark practices and procedures in India was identified as early as the 19th century, and it was fulfilled with the enactment of the Trademarks Act of 1940. Since then, Indian trademark law has continued to evolve in harmony with the nation's rapidly changing and modernizing economy. Currently, the Trademarks Act of 1999 governs national trademark practices in India.

Meaning and Definitions

Following are few key definitions from the Indian Trademarks Act.

"**Trademark** means a mark capable of being represented graphically and which is capable of distinguishing the goods or services of one person from those of another and mat include shape of goods, their packaging and combination of colours" (Sec 2 (Zb)).

"**Appellate Board**" means the Appellate Board established under section 83.

"**Assignment**" means an assignment in writing by act of the parties concerned.

"**Associated trademarks**" means trademarks deemed to be, or required to be, registered as associated trademarks under this Act.

"**Bench**" means a Bench of the Appellate Board, signs and symbols, design, expression, tagline, logo, abbreviation.

Object of Trademark

The main purpose of a trademark is to identify the origin of the goods, not to describe the characteristics of the goods. So, the primary objective of trademark protection is to serve the interests of both businesses and consumers in the marketplace. Trademarks play a crucial role in achieving several key objectives:

Identification of Source: Trademarks are distinctive symbols, names, or other identifiers that allow consumers to easily recognize and identify the source of a particular product or service. They help consumers make informed choices by providing assurance of the product's origin and quality.

Consumer Protection: Trademarks protect consumers from confusion and deception. When consumers see a trademark they recognize, they can have confidence that the product or service they are purchasing is genuine and meets certain quality standards. This reduces the risk of consumers being misled or purchasing inferior or counterfeit products.

Brand Recognition and Loyalty: Trademarks help businesses build and promote their brands. A strong trademark can become synonymous with a company's reputation for quality and excellence. Over time, this can lead to brand loyalty among consumers who prefer products associated with a particular trademark.

Incentive for Innovation: Trademark protection provides an incentive for businesses to invest in the development and promotion of new products and services. Knowing that their trademarks are legally protected, businesses are more likely to invest in innovation and quality to maintain their brand's reputation.

Fair Competition: Trademarks promote fair competition by preventing unauthorized parties from using similar marks that could confuse consumers. This ensures that businesses can compete in the marketplace based on the merits of their products and services rather than through deceptive practices.

Asset Value: Trademarks are valuable assets for businesses. They can be bought, sold, licensed, and used as collateral for loans. Strong and well-recognized trademarks can significantly enhance a company's overall value.

Legal Recourse: Trademarks provide legal remedies to trademark owners in case of infringement. Owners can take legal action against those who use their trademarks without authorization, seek damages, and obtain injunctions to stop further infringement.

Consumer Trust: Trademarks build trust and confidence among consumers. Over time, a successful trademark becomes associated with a certain level of quality and reliability, which can lead to repeat business and positive word-of-mouth marketing.

Go Global: Trademarks facilitate global expansion for businesses by allowing them to establish a consistent brand identity across different countries. International trademark registration systems, such as the Madrid Protocol, make it easier for businesses to protect their trademarks globally.

In summary, the primary objective of trademark protection is to create a fair and orderly marketplace where consumers can make informed choices, businesses can build and protect their brand identities, and innovation is encouraged. Trademarks serve as a bridge of trust between consumers and businesses, promoting healthy competition and economic growth.

Madrid Protocol on Trademarks

The Madrid Protocol, also known as the Madrid System, is an international treaty that simplifies and streamlines the process of trademark registration and management across multiple countries. It is administered by the World Intellectual Property Organization (WIPO), a specialized agency of the United Nations. Key features of the protocol are centralized filing & management, designation of member countries in the trademark application,

Features of Good Trademark

Trademarks give a brand image and creates a trust in the minds of customers. So, a good trademark is a critical asset for any business. It helps in distinguishing products or services from competitors, builds brand recognition, and fosters consumer trust. To be effective and legally protectable, a trademark should possess certain following features:

Distinctiveness: A strong trademark should be distinctive and capable of setting your product or service apart from others in the marketplace. Distinctiveness can be achieved through unique names, symbols, or designs.

Uniqueness: Your trademark should not be generic or descriptive of the product or service you offer. Generic terms or phrases cannot be registered as trademarks because they are considered common and not distinctive.

Memorability: A good trademark should be easy to remember, making it more likely that consumers will recall your brand when making purchasing decisions. Memorable trademarks are often simple and uncomplicated.

Suggestiveness: While not outright descriptive, a suggestive trademark indirectly conveys some aspect of the product or service. These can be strong and memorable if they require consumers to make a connection between the mark and the product or service.

Non-descriptiveness: A trademark should avoid describing the features, characteristics, or ingredients of the product or service. Descriptive terms or phrases are weak trademarks.

Arbitrariness: An arbitrary trademark uses a word or symbol that has no direct connection to the product or service it represents. These can be highly distinctive and memorable.

Fancifulness: Fanciful trademarks are entirely made-up words or symbols with no preexisting meaning. These are often the strongest and most protectable trademarks.

Visual Appeal: Visual elements, such as logos or design elements, should be aesthetically pleasing and visually memorable. They should be versatile and adaptable to different media and sizes.

Phonetic Appeal: Trademarks should sound pleasing and be easy to pronounce, as this aids in word-of-mouth recognition and recall.

Legal Protectability: Ensure that your trademark is legally protectable by conducting a comprehensive trademark search to ensure it is not already in use by others. It should also be eligible for trademark registration under applicable laws.

Broad Applicability: A good trademark should allow for brand extensions and be suitable for use across various product lines or services.

Longevity: Ideally, a trademark should have enduring appeal and not be subject to trends that may become outdated quickly.

Cultural Sensitivity: Consider cultural connotations and sensitivities associated with your trademark, especially if you plan to expand internationally.

Avoiding Offensive or Controversial Elements: Be cautious about using elements in your trademark that could be offensive or controversial, as they may alienate potential customers.

Distinctive Colours: If using color in your trademark, choose distinctive and unique colours that are not commonly associated with your industry.

Protection against Infringement: Ensure that your trademark is strong enough to protect against potential infringement by others, as well as dilution of your brand's distinctiveness.

Creating a good trademark is a crucial aspect of brand development and protection. It is often advisable to collaborate with legal professionals or trademark experts to navigate the complexities of trademark law and registration to ensure that your trademark possesses these key features and is legally protectable.

Types of Trademarks

The following are types of trademarks.

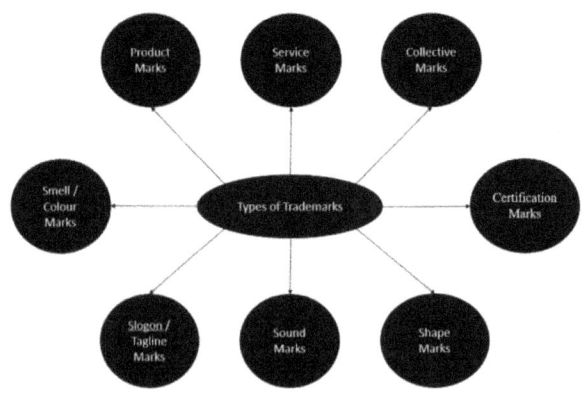

Product Marks: A product mark is used for products or goods, not for services. This type of mark serves to identify a product's origin and contributes to maintaining a company's reputation. Trademark applications filed in trademark classes 1-34 are often referred to as product marks because they pertain to goods. A product mark is affixed to a product or good to distinguish its identity from others. Examples include well-known brands like **Bata and Amul**.

Product marks can fall into one of the following categories: Generic Marks, Descriptive Marks, Suggestive Marks, Fanciful Marks, or arbitrary Marks.

Services Marks: A service mark is a brand name or logo that identifies a service provider. Service marks encompass words, phrases, symbols, designs, or combinations of these elements. As a form of intellectual property protection, service marks prevent competitors from using names and insignia that may confuse consumers. They distinguish the services of one proprietor or owner from those of other companies providing services such as computer hardware and software assembly, restaurant and hotel services, courier and transport, beauty and healthcare, advertising, publishing, and more. This protection helps safeguard their names and marks from being misused by others. Examples include **Yahoo and Google**.

Collective Mark: According to Section 2 (g), a "collective trademark" refers to a trademark that distinguishes the goods or services of members of an association of persons (excluding partnerships as defined in the Indian Partnership Act, 1932), which is the proprietor of the mark, from those of others.

A collective mark is owned by an association and used by its members. Examples of collective marks include "**Chartered Accountant (CA),**" "**Company Secretaries (CS),**" and "**Certified Public Accountant (CPA).**" Collective marks serve to inform the public about specific characteristics of the products for which the collective mark is used. Collective trademarks are an exception to the underlying principle that trademarks can be exclusively owned and used by their owner.

Certification Marks: A certification mark (also known as a mark of conformity, mark of validity, or mark of trust) is a commercial product that indicates that the manufacturer of the product has tested and verified strict compliance with certain predetermined quality standards during manufacturing. is a specific mark of the product. Again, each specific certification mark may also indicate the product's origin, materials of manufacture or construction, manufacturing process or method, purity or precision, or specific characteristics of the product.

For instance, the **ISI (Indian Standard Institute) mark** is a certification mark. Another example is the CII (Confederation of Indian Industry) mark.

The following are the most famous State enforced (statutory) **certification marks issued for various products in India**, informed here to help the people and economic entities concerned:

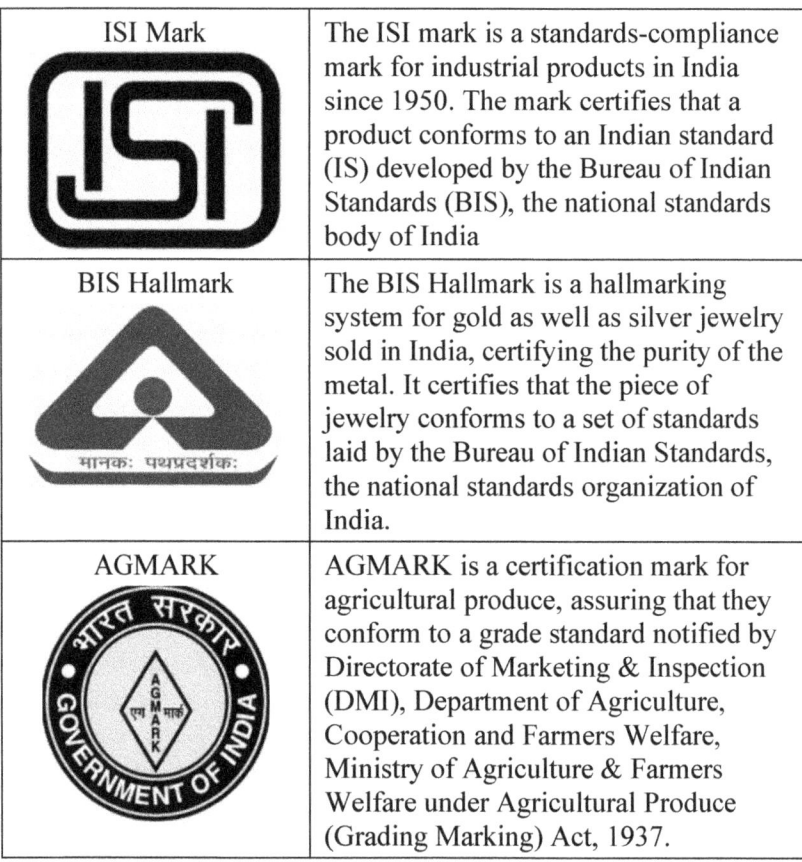

ISI Mark	The ISI mark is a standards-compliance mark for industrial products in India since 1950. The mark certifies that a product conforms to an Indian standard (IS) developed by the Bureau of Indian Standards (BIS), the national standards body of India
BIS Hallmark	The BIS Hallmark is a hallmarking system for gold as well as silver jewelry sold in India, certifying the purity of the metal. It certifies that the piece of jewelry conforms to a set of standards laid by the Bureau of Indian Standards, the national standards organization of India.
AGMARK	AGMARK is a certification mark for agricultural produce, assuring that they conform to a grade standard notified by Directorate of Marketing & Inspection (DMI), Department of Agriculture, Cooperation and Farmers Welfare, Ministry of Agriculture & Farmers Welfare under Agricultural Produce (Grading Marking) Act, 1937.

Intellectual Property Rights - 1

FPO Mark 	The FPO mark is a certification mark mandatory on all processed fruit products sold in India such as packaged fruit beverages, fruit-jams, squashes, pickles, dehydrated fruit products, and fruit extracts, following the Food Safety and Standards Act of 2006.	

Many other certifications mark in India are - India Organic, Non-polluting vehicle, Eco mark, Vegetarian etc.

Collective Marks Vs Certification Marks:

Differentiator	Collective Marks	Certification Marks
Owner	Collective marks are owned by associations, groups, or organizations formed by individuals, businesses, or other entities. These organizations typically consist of members who share a common characteristic, such as a trade association or a collective of producers.	Certification marks are owned by an entity or organization that is independent of the producers or service providers using the mark. This entity is responsible for certifying and verifying that the products or services bearing the mark meet specific established standards.
Usage	Collective marks are used by members of the association to indicate that their products or services meet certain defined standards or criteria set by the association. The mark serves as a	Certification marks are used by producers or service providers to signify that their products or services conform to certain predefined standards, quality, or characteristics. The mark indicates that an independent certifying

		badge of affiliation with the group.	body has verified compliance
	Control	The association that owns the collective mark exercises control over its use. This control may involve establishing specific quality or authenticity standards that members must adhere to when using the mark	The owner of a certification mark maintains strict control over its use. They set the standards and criteria that products or services must meet to use the mark and may conduct regular inspections or evaluations
	Consumer Information	Collective marks inform consumers that the products or services bearing the mark meet specific criteria or standards associated with the group. They provide consumers with confidence in the quality or characteristics of the products or services.	Certification marks provide consumers with assurance that the products or services they purchase meet specific quality or safety standards. Consumers can trust that an independent organization has verified the product or service's attributes.
	Examples	Examples of collective marks include "Chartered Accountant (CA)," "Company Secretaries (CS)," and "Certified Public Accountant (CPA)." These marks indicate that the professionals using them are members of the respective professional associations	Examples of certification marks include "ISO 9001" (International Organization for Standardization) for quality management systems, "USDA Organic" for organic products, and "CE" for conformity with European Union standards

Shape Marks: According to Article 3 (3) (c) EUTMIR, a shape mark is a trademark that consists of a three-dimensional shape, including containers, packaging, the product itself or its appearance. When the shape of goods, packaging has some distinctive feature it can be registered. 3D shape or design is also protected under Trademark law. E.g. Shape of the Coke bottle, Shape of Kit-Kat Chocolate. In India also shape marks are approve except in the following cases:

- **Non-Distinctive Shapes:** Shape marks that are purely functional or lack distinctiveness may be refused registration. A shape that is commonly used in the industry to serve a functional purpose and does not inherently identify the source of goods or services may not qualify for registration.

- **Shapes That Are Generic or Descriptive:** Shapes that are generic or merely descriptive of the product or its characteristics are not eligible for trademark registration. These shapes do not function as source indicators.

- **Shapes That Have Become Customary:** If a shape has become customary in the relevant trade, it may not be registrable as a trademark. In other words, if the shape is commonly used by competitors in the industry, it may not be distinctive enough to serve as a trademark.

- **Functional Shapes:** Shapes that are purely functional, serving a utilitarian purpose, are not eligible for trademark protection. Protection for functional features is typically sought through patents or design registrations.

- **Shapes That Are Deceptive:** Shapes that are likely to deceive or cause confusion among consumers regarding the nature, quality, or origin of the goods may not be registrable.

- **Shapes That Violate Public Morality or Order:** Shapes that are contrary to public morality or order may be refused registration. Offensive or scandalous shapes would fall into this category.

Sound Marks: A sound mark is a trademark where a specific sound uniquely identifies the origin of a product or service. Examples include the Airtel Jingle, MGM's Roar of the Lion, Yahoo Yodel, and Nokia Tune.

The European Union has also granted sound marks for non-musical sounds, such as Tarzan's Yelling and MGM Roar. Sound trademarks use sound to uniquely identify commercial sources of goods and services. In recent years, sound marks have gained popularity in the market as a brand not bound by tradition. Sound helps identify the origin of a product or service.

Slogans or Taglines: While the terms "slogan" and "tagline" are often used interchangeably, there is a subtle difference between the two. A slogan conveys a company's mission statement, while a tagline evokes the brand's image. Slogans are more advertising-oriented, whereas taglines are more publicity-oriented. Slogans are used to sell products, while taglines raise overall brand awareness. Taglines are also considered trademarks when used along with other business marks. Examples include McDonald's "I'm Lovin' It," LIC's "Zindagi Ke Saath Bhi, Zindagi Ke Baad Bhi," and Nike's "Just Do It."

Smell Marks / Olfactory: An olfactory mark identifies a product by its odour. They are more challenging to register than sound marks because they lack a visual form of expression. Graphical representation is a requirement for trademark registration, making it difficult for smell marks to meet this criterion. For example, in the UK, Sumitomo Rubber Co. was granted a smell mark for a rose scent, but a request for a cinnamon smell mark in furniture was rejected in the Ralf Seickman case in Germany. In India, smell marks are not recognized.

Color Marks: A color mark uses one or more colors to uniquely identify the commercial source of a product or service. Registering a particular color or color combination as a trademark can be challenging. For instance, Germany awarded its first color trademark, and in the US, Corning Fiber Glass Corporation obtained a pink color trademark for home insulation after a lengthy legal battle. In India, under exceptional circumstances, a single color may be allowed as a trademark if it can demonstrate its uniqueness to consumers. An example is the Bisleri brand's color mark, which has been trademarked despite several deceptively similar brands.

The Indian Trademarks Act, 1999

The Indian Trademarks Act, 1999, governs trademark registration and protection in India. It provides the legal framework for the registration, use, and protection of trademarks in the country. Here are some key provisions and aspects of the Indian Trademarks Act:

- **Definition of Trademark:** The Act defines a trademark as any mark capable of being represented graphically and distinguishing the goods or services of one person from those of others. It includes marks in the form of words, names, symbols, devices, or a combination there of.

- **Registration of Trademarks:** The Act allows for the registration of trademarks to confer exclusive rights to the owner to use the mark in connection with specific goods or services.

- **Absolute and Relative Grounds for Refusal:** The Act outlines absolute and relative grounds for refusing trademark registration. Absolute grounds include marks that are devoid of distinctive character, generic, descriptive, or customary in the trade. Relative grounds include conflicts with earlier trademarks or other rights.

- **Examination and Opposition:** Trademark applications undergo examination by the Trademarks Office, and third parties can file oppositions against applications if they believe there are valid grounds for refusal.

- **Classification of Goods and Services:** The Act follows the Nice Classification system, which categorizes goods and services into specific classes for trademark registration purposes.

- **Duration and Renewal:** Trademark registrations in India are initially valid for ten years from the date of application. Registrations can be renewed indefinitely for successive ten-year periods.

- **Infringement and Enforcement:** The Act provides remedies and procedures for trademark infringement, including civil and criminal actions, injunctions, and damages.

- **Collective Marks and Certification Marks:** The Act allows for the registration of collective marks and certification marks. Collective marks are owned by associations or groups of persons and indicate a common origin, while certification marks certify the quality, origin, or other characteristics of goods or services.

- **Well-Known Trademarks:** The Act recognizes the concept of well-known trademarks and provides protection against their dilution or infringement.

- **Geographical Indications:** While not related to trademarks, the Act also addresses geographical indications (GIs) to protect products originating from specific regions known for their unique characteristics.

- **International Treaties:** India is a signatory to international treaties related to trademarks, including the Paris Convention and the Madrid Protocol, which allow for international trademark protection.

- **Amendments:** The Trademarks Act has undergone amendments over the years to align with international standards and address emerging issues related to trademark registration and protection.

The Indian Trade

marks Act plays a crucial role in safeguarding intellectual property rights and promoting fair competition in the Indian marketplace. It provides legal protection to trademark owners and helps consumers make informed choices by ensuring the authenticity and quality of products and services.

Trademarks Registration

Register a trademark, a trademark application must be filed in India with the Registrar of Trademarks. Branding makes it easier for your customer base to find you. Brands differentiate your services and products from those of your competitors. This identifies you as the source and demonstrates a consistent level of quality in our services and products. Brands also increase brand awareness and goodwill.

Two basic requirements of trademark registrations are.

a. The mark can be presented graphically either in paper form or digital form.

b. Is capable of distinguishing goods or services from others.

The procedure for registration of Trademark is:

1. Application for registration of Trademark is to be made u/s 18 of the Act.
2. The application is advertised as per u/s 20 of the Act.
3. Any person may file an opposition u/s 21, within 4 months from advertisement of Trademark application.
4. The applicant is entitled to correct any error, remove the opposition, or make any amendment u/s 22 of the Act.
5. The registrar is entitled to registration for the trademark withing 18 months from the date of filing of application u/s 23.

If any trademark application is not completed within 12 months from the date of filing of application, it is deemed to be abandoned.

Registered Trademark:

A registered trademark is a trademark that can be represented graphically and that can be distinguished from the goods and services of others. Registrable trademarks under the TRIPS Agreement state that "any sign or combination of signs capable of distinguishing the goods or services of one company from those of another company may constitute a trademark".

Advantages of Registered Trademark

Trademark applications can be filed for registrable marks.

1. Multiple Country Recognition.
2. Ownership: Only registered users can use it.
3. Popularity.
4. Reduces the possibility of disputes.

5. Easy to burden of proof.

6. Exclusive rights in commercial activities.

Is Registration Mandatory?

Distinctive marks to enjoy exclusive rights with respect to its use even without registration. If registered, then it is easy to prove that Trademark is owned by the company.

Non-Registrable Marks:

A trademark that cannot be registered as a trademark as it is not sufficiently distinguished from other trademarks is called an unregistered trademark. This meant that the brand was unable to differentiate itself from other goods and services. Therefore, a trademark that cannot be registered cannot be registered as a trademark.

- Trademarks not recognized under the Trademark Act.
- Trademarks that mislead or confuse the public.
- Trademarks consist of matters offending the religious sensibility of any class or section of Indian citizens.
- Brands with inappropriate or vulgar content.
- Trademarks prohibited by the Unauthorized Use Act 1950. A feature of a product is the shape that is directly attributable to the nature of the product.
- Trademarks where shape is important for technical results.
- Trademarks that are similar in identity to other goods or products.

Basic Principles of Registered Trademark

- Invented words or phrases of a trademark must not directly describe the nature or quality of goods and services.
- A character can be a combination of letters or numbers. Brands may use flashy devices and symbols.
- Symbols can be represented as monograms.
- You can combine multiple color combinations or specific colors with words or devices.
- Consider the shape of the product and the specific packaging of the product.
- These markings form a three-dimensional character. An audible signal that can be represented by a standard system or described in words for graphical representation.

Deceptive Similarity:

"Deceptively similarity" trademark is a concept which can be understood as a brand that resembles or appears to be like an existing brand to deceive and confuse customers. This deceptive similarity concept was debated in the Trademarks Act 1999. Under section 2 (h) of the Act, a mark is classified as another mark if it appears like, or is likely to be confused with, another mark. must be viewed as deceptively similar.

Assignment and Transmission

Assignment and Transmission of Trademark is a process of transferring ownership of a trademark from one person to another with full or partial rights, depending on the terms of the trademark owner. Registered and unregistered trademarks may be assigned and assigned from one person to another with or without the good faith of the affiliates.

Generally, Assignment and Transmission are used interchangeably. Whereas Section 2 of the Trademark Act 1999 clearly differentiates between the two. trademark assignment, the ownership of the registered trademark is changed, in case of assignment, the rights to the trademark remain with the original owner, but only limited right to use the trademark/brand is passed to a third party.

Rectification of Register

Section 57 of the Trademarks Act, 1999 provides for the grounds for Rectification of the Register. An application for Rectification or cancellation of a trademark can be made so that the trademark is not used for a certain period after the trademark is registered.

Functions of Trademark

Trademark plays key role in building products brand image and building confidence in the buyer to go and grab the product.

Origin: It is a statutory privilege granted by the government to inventors and to other persons deriving their rights from the inventor for fixed years to exclude other persons from manufacturing, using, or selling a patented product or processes

Choice: Trademark means a mark capable of being represented graphically and which can distinguish the goods or services of one person from those of other and may include shape of goods, their packaging and combination of colours (section 2 (zb) of Trademark Act, 1999)

Quality: Trademark provides confidence to the customer about the quality of the product and brings in repeat business.

Marketing: Trademark distinguishes one company product from other company. Once registered trademarks will be valid for 10 years and can be renewed any number of times every 10 years.

Eg. Pepsi is a trademark of Pepsi Co for its cola drink, same way Coca Cola is a registered trademark of Coca cola Inc.

Economic: these are indications which identify a goods as originating in the territory of a member, or a region or locality in that territory, where a given quality, reputation, or other characteristics of the good is attributable to geographic region. The purpose of this identification is to protect customers from buying fake Geographically indications tagged product.

Eg: Mysore Silk Sarees: This tag is associated with Karnataka Silk Industries Corporation (KSIC), and one should use this tag other than KSIC.

> Modern trademark laws view trademarks as serving three distinct functions:
> 1. They indicate the origin or owner of the item to which they are attached.
> 2. They guarantee that these products meet certain quality standards.
> 3. Promote the item that symbolizes.

Duration

- The trademark registered is valid for a period of 10 years.
- It can be further renewed for a term of 10 years for unlimited times.
- The failure to renew the trademark within the stipulated period, a grace period of maximum 1 year granted for restoration of the trademark.

Absolute Grounds for refusal – Section-9

Trademarks only be registered if they are distinctive and not descriptive. Following are the grounds for refusal of issuance of Trademark.

1. Should not create confusion.
2. Should not be devoid of distinctiveness.
3. If anything becomes customary in the current language.
4. Should not be hurt religious sentiment.
5. Should not be obscene.
6. Names protect under Emblem and names.

7. If shape of trademark derives for goods itself.

Case: Amrithadhara Pharmacy Vs Satya Deo Gupta.

"Act doesn't lay down any criteria for determining what is likely to deceive or confusion, every case must depend on its own particular fact."

Cases:
1. L&T Ltd Vs LNT.
2. Cadila Health Vs Cadila Pharmaceuticals.

Relative Ground of Refusal (Section-11).

If the marks are same or similar in relation to earlier marks, then it can be refused.

Rights conferred by registration - Section-28

Section 28 deals with the rights conferred by registration. It gives the exclusive right to use the trademark in relation to its goods or services.

Well-known Marks

Marks which has become so to the substantial segment of the public which uses such goods or services, that the use of such mark in relation to other goods or services would be likely to be taken as indicating a connection in the course of trade or rendering of services between these goods or services and a person using the mark in relation to the first mentioned goods or serves.

Key points
1. Substantial segment of the public use e.g.: TATA.
2. Used by another person e.g., TATA diamonds This indicates connection between TATA Group and TATA diamonds.

There are around eighty-one well-known trademarks in India.

Globally recognized well–known trademarks are – Google, Amul, Apple etc.

Section 11 (2) protects the well-known trademarks.

Criteria to protect well-known marks.

1. The number of persons involved in the claim of goods & services.
2. Number of people who know about the organization.
3. Number of consumers buying the product.
4. The extent or geographical boundaries of operation.
5. How often is it bought by customer?

Application to be submitted onsite ipcindia.nic.in.

The following are not pre-requisite.

1. That tie trademark has been used in India.
2. That the trademark has been recognized.
3. That the application is filed in India.

Distinctiveness of Trademark

It is important to note that trademarks must have certain characteristics to get benefit of remedies.

1. **Not distinctive or generic words** cannot be protected. In the case of Bharath Pe Vs Phone Pe where the word "Pe" used by Bharath Pe was objected to by Phone Pe. It is held that "Pe" word is a generic word and does not warrant protection, so word "Pe" used in Bharath Pe is valid.

2. **Descriptive:** Term or symbol identifies attributes of the product such as purpose, size, color etc. cannot be protected. Merely descriptive does not qualify for protection. Qualify for protection mark must acquire a secondary meaning. A surname incorporated into a mark is treated as a descriptive mark and does not quality for protection.

    Eg: Mc. Donald, Hilton Hotels, Adigas Hotels etc.

3. **Subjective:** It does not describe the product; it suggests the nature of characteristics. The product must still bear some relationship with the mark. These qualifies for protection.

   Eg: Nissan SUV name – Pathfinder.

4. **Arbitrary and fanciful:** Trademark which do not suggest or describe any characteristics of production is called as Arbitrary and fanciful trademarks. Product is more likely to be associated with symbols. These are eligible for the strongest protection.

   Eg: Apple Computer, Yamaha Motorcycle.

Few more points

1. Using the Geographical origin of goods in trademark is prohibited.
2. Only marks which have the capability of distinguishing can be registered.

Offences and Penalties

Section 114 regulates crimes committed by companies under the Act. If a company creates something remarkably like another company's trademark and this causes consumer confusion, it will be considered guilty unless it proves innocence or ignorance and punished accordingly.

Penalties for Trademark Infringement: -

1. **Section 103:** If a person is found to be counterfeiting an existing trademark or trade name and applying his own goods or services, he shall be punished with imprisonment of 6 months to 3 years and a fine of Rs.5 lakh, Rs.2 lakh. be imposed.

2. **Article 104:** If you are found selling or renting goods or services with false trademarks or descriptions attached, you will be subject to the same penalties as above.

3. **Section 105:** If a person previously convicted of the offences prescribed in sections 103 and 104 is again found guilty of those offences, he will be punishable for every subsequent offence with

4. **Section 106:** If you sell or exhibit for sale any of the premises referred to in Section 81, or hold for sale or commercial purposes, or for the manufacture of cloth or cotton yarn or cotton yarn. If anything, not stipulated in this section is marked as stipulated, all such pieces and bundles of yarn and all such yarn and those used in its wrapping shall be returned to the Government for a fee of up to Rs. shall be fined.

5. **Section 107:** No one may misrepresent a trademark as being legally registered and, if convicted, faces up to three years in prison or a fine, or possibly both.

6. **Section 108:** If someone falsely states that their branch is officially affiliated with the Trademark Office, that person is punishable by up to two years in prison and/or a fine.

7. **Section 109:** Anyone who makes a false entry in the register is punishable by up to two years' imprisonment, a fine, or both.

- Coca-Cola Company vs. Bisleri International Pvt Ltd:
- Sony Corporation vs. K. Selvamurthy:

Domain Name

A domain name is a user-friendly way of specifying an Internet Protocol address. Domain names are commonly used to find product and service websites where consumers want to view information about products and services. It is the online identity of a particular person, creation, or organization. A domain name is the online address of a person, entity, or organization that leads to the page that the public wants to see when they enter the domain name.

Businesses and companies commonly use a business name or trade name that they use as their online identity or domain name when doing business. A permanent address that can be accessed from anywhere in the world, regardless of the location of the domain name owner. A domain name registration thus gives a person's or an organization's online identity a worldwide presence.

Domain names are formed according to the rules and conventions laid down in the Domain Name System. All names registered in the Domain Name System are domain names. There is only a minimal number of domains available. Examples include "org" for organizations (non-profit), "gov" for government agencies, "edu" for educational institutions, and "com" for commercial companies. Domain names are website addresses which people use to access the website (eg.www.google.com, www.flipkart.com). Exist in the virtual world all business will have to register a domain name which acts as an online address through which they can connect and communicate with their customers.

Domain Names

Indian Trademark law protects domain names as distinct trademark, and it is demonstrated in landmark cases (details of domain name is discussed in Chapter-6)

Tatsons Ltd Vs Manu Kosuri & ors
Yahoo Inc Vs Ashok Arora

The mandatory requirements for domain name branding in India?

- Domain names must be unique.

- Domain names should not be offensive.

- A domain name should identify your company's products and services and distinguish it from other companies in the market.

- The domain name must not infringe any registered or pending trademarks.

After all the necessary conditions are met, the domain name owner can apply for trademark registration of the domain name along with all the required documents.

Registering Domain Names

Registration of domain name undertaken by the Internet Corporation for Assigned Names and Numbers (ICANN), a no profit institution. The basis for granting domain name is not based on the requirements stated in the trademark legislation. Registration is based on the first to apply basis. This has given rise to multiple issues like cybersquatting and frivolous disputes.

Resolving Domain Name disputes

Domain name dispute can be resolved through Uniform Dispute Resolution Policy (UDRP) set by ICANN.

1. Similar or identical to a trademark.
2. Registered in the absence of good faith.
3. No legitimate interest.

Traditional passing off suit may also be brought in Indian court.

Case: Satyam Info way Vs Sify net solutions.

Go Daddy Vs Academy Awards

Case: Novartis Case on Evergreen Patentability

Extending patent over 20 years with slightly altered or different version is not considered as invention. Getting patents renewed with small modification leads to evergreen patentability. So, invention should be significantly different than the present art.

Trademark related cases

1. Coca Cola Vs Bisleri.
2. Whatman International Ltd Vs P. Mehta.
3. Starbucks Vs Sardar Baksh.
4. Yahoo Inc Vs Akash Arora.
5. Zara fashions Vs Zara food.

6. Academy Awards Vs. Go Daddy.

7. Amul Vs Amuldistributors.com.

Remedies

Obtaining a domain name trademark in India protects the trademark owner from infringement just like any other kind of trademark. In the event of domain name trademark infringement in India, domain name owners may take the following actions: Trademark infringement in India is a crime that many people are willing to commit. Criminals believe that no one will notice. And if your business fell victim to these criminals, they were right - you do not realize it. And you will not notice it right away. You cannot live in fear because you have a job to take care of. But once you notice a violation, you can do something about it.

Remedies available to the Owner of Trademark of Domain Name in India:

1. Trademark Infringement.
2. Passing Off.

Trademark Infringement

Trademark protected under Trademark Act,1999. Infringement of a trademark in India means a violation of the exclusive right that are granted to the proprietor registered under the Trademarks Act,1999. Rights are confirmed by registration mentioned in section - 28.

Section - 29 states that violation of rights specified in Section - 28 is called infringement.

Section - 30 states the situation when a registered trademark does not constitute infringement.

What Constitutes Infringement?

An unauthorized person uses a trademark that is identical or deceptively like a registered trademark is known as infringement.

Kinds of Infringement

1. Direct Infringement
2. Indirect Infringement

Direct Infringement

The following acts constitute Direct infringement.

1. The registered trademark is used by any unauthorized person without a license from the owner.
2. Identical / Deceptive Similarity: The mark used deceptively similar or identical with the mark in dispute. It can cause confusion in the minds of the public to have an association with the registered trademark. There is a change for a likelihood of confusion among the public. If the consumers are likely to get confused between the two marks, then there is an infringement.

Eg:

Larsen & Turbo Ltd (L&T) Vs Laxmi Narain Traders (LNT).

Cadila Health Vs Cadila Pharmaceuticals.

1. A person uses a registered mark means.

a. Affixes it to goods or the packaging thereof.
b. Offers or exposes goods for sales and puts them on the market or stocks them for those purposes under the registered trademarks.
c. Imports or exports goods under the mark; or
d. Uses the registered trademark for business purposes or in advertising.

Indirect Infringement

Any other form infringement other than points or ways mentioned in direct infringement is called as Indirect infringement. Following are the instances of Indirect infringement.

1. When a person induces the direct infringer to commit the infringement, it is called indirect infringement or contributory infringement.
2. When the person can control the action of the direct infringer.
3. When a person derives a financial benefit from the infringement.
4. When a person has knowledge of the infringement and contributes to it. The person is said to be vicariously liable.

The remedies for trademark infringement are:

Filing an Injunction Against Trademark Use:

If you catch someone using your trademark, an injunction can stop them immediately. The court will issue an injunction. Get a Trademark Attorney. File a case to receive a residence order. The court then orders the trademark infringer to stop using the trademark.

Even if the lawsuit is not resolved immediately, the injunction will prevent the infringer from using your trademark or anything like your trademark.

Claim damages:

What is your brand this another person has been using for so long? Think of all the money you might have lost in the meantime. File a lawsuit seeking damages. The damages cover your attorney fees and give you additional money to cover any damage to your reputation that may have been caused. Victims of trademark infringement always seek damages.

Request Profits:

What if your brand thief was in the same business as you? He/she pretended to be you to attract your customers to him/her. is to find out how much you earned. If that real money was made by misleading customers, you have the right to do anything.

Making a profit from a transaction that misuses your name can be difficult. Get the best trademark attorney for that.

Storage and Sealing of Infringing Material:

The court will seize and seal the infringing material and suspend future use, among other remedies.

When a trademark is said to be infringed, both civil and criminal action can be bought against the wrongdoer.

Civil remedies

The competent jurisdiction can give the following if the infringement is successfully proved.

- a. Injunction / Stay.
- b. Appropriate damages.
- c. Handing over of accounts & profits.
- d. Appointment of a local commissioner by respective court for custody or sealing of infringing material & accounts.
- e. An application under order 39 Rule 1&2 of CPC for grant of temporary or ad interim ex-parte injunction.

Criminal Remedies

Chapter XII of the Act deals with the offences, penalties, and procedure.

Section 103 & 104 provide for imprisonment for a term not less than six months which may be extended up to 3 years and fine not less than fifty thousand rupees which may extend up to 2 Lakh rupees.

The provision for enhancement of punishment is laid down u/s 105 of Trademarks Act,1999.

Passing off

Section 27 (1) states that no action for infringement can be taken for unregistered trademark.

Section 27 (2) states that there is an alternative remedy available for unregistered trademarks. It is called as passing off.

Claim remedies under passing off, following three conditions must be fulfilled.

1. The trademark has a reputation.
2. There was misrepresentation.
3. It has caused injury or loss.

Key Case Studies - Trademark

Plaintiff: Satyam Info way Ltd.

Defendant: Sify net Solutions Pvt. Ltd.

Date decided: 6 May 2004

Ruling court: Supreme Court of India.

Decision by: RUMA PAL & P. VENKATARAMA REDDI.

Citation(s): 2004 (3) AWC 2366 SC.

In the case, Satyam Infoway accused Sifynet Solutions of attempting to impersonate its service by incorporating similar words in its domain name, creating potential confusion among consumers. This marked a significant domain name protection case in India involving companies using variations of the same trademark, "Sify." Satyam Infoway argued that Sifynet Solutions' actions could lead consumers to mistakenly believe that the latter was affiliated with Satyam Infoway.

An appeal was made to the Supreme Court after the complainant used the term "Sify" in its domain name, raising suspicions among customers and prompting the appellant to seek a provisional injunction.

The final judgment, delivered by a panel of Justices Ruma Pal and P. Venkatarama Reddi, overturned the High Court's decision, ruling in favor of Satyam Infoway. The Supreme Court clarified that domain names fall under the legal framework of trademarks, despite the absence of specific regulations for domain names in India. The judgment emphasized that domain names are protected under the Trademarks Act of 1999, addressing issues related to passing off.

2. Yahoo Inc Vs. Akash Arora.

Case Title: Yahoo!, Inc vs Akash Arora & Anr,

Petitioner: Yahoo! Inc.

Respondent: Akash Arora and ANR.

Ruling Court: Delhi High court.

Date of Judgement: 19 February 1999.

Citation: 1999 IIAD Delhi 229, 78 (1999) DLT 285.

In a dispute involving domain names, one party owned 'Yahoo,' while the defendant possessed 'Yahoo India.' The court was asked to consider the modern web consumer's awareness. The court held that even an experienced internet user might be an inexperienced information consumer and could mistake the defendant's site for the plaintiffs. The final judgment favored the plaintiff, stating that the use of a brand name resembling another company's could cause confusion and harm. The court issued an injunction, prohibiting the defendant from conducting business, selling services, or using the domain name "Yahooindia.com" or similar brands, emphasizing the plaintiff's pending trademark dispute resolution.

Casio India Co. Ltd Vs. Ashita Tele Systems:

Petitioner: Casio India Co. Ltd.

Respondent: Ashita Tele Systems.

Citation: Appeal No. 6564 of 2002.

Judgement: On, 08 September 2003.

Ruling Court: High Court of Delhi.

Judges: The Honorable Mr. Justice Manmohan Sarin.

For the Appearing Parties: Sanjay Jain, Shyarn Murjani, Advocates.

In this case, preliminary objections were raised, contending that Mumbai, not Delhi, should have jurisdiction for the lawsuit against Casio India, a Mumbai-based company. The court ruled that territorial jurisdiction challenges should be evaluated considering the broader context of information technology advancements rather than conventionally. The accessibility of the website's domain name elsewhere was a crucial factor, expanding the authority beyond the defendant's residential location. The judgment favored the plaintiffs, noting sufficient prima facie evidence for an injunction. Convenience considerations favored the plaintiff, leading to a prohibition on the defendant from using the "CASIO" trademark and brand name on the website 'www.casioindia.com', except without the word "CASIO."

Summary

- A trademark registration establishes ownership of a trademark, name, or logo. Protect your brand against illegal use by third parties.
- Trademarks are primarily used to identify the source or source of goods, products, or services.
- Trademarks can distinguish the goods or services of one person or company from others. They are Indian intellectual property rights.
- The Trademarks Act 1999 regulates the registration and functioning of trademarks. India is a huge competitive market for business and company owners with many new but identical brands/products appearing every day. To prevent this is where it becomes necessary to protect your trademark.
- Trademark registration is a legal process regulated by the Trademarks Act 1999. Your brand can prove to be an effective and simple communication tool. you speak for yourself.
- It governs the use, creation and protection of intellectual property rights and other established legal rights related to trademarks. Trademark law is part of Intellectual Property Rights (IPR).
- Some Important Trademark Treaties
    - Paris Convention
    - TRIPS Agreement
    - Trademark Law Treaty
    - Singapore Trademark Law Treaty

Intellectual Property Rights - 1

- Madrid Protocol

Questions

1. What is the term of a registered trademark?
2. Trace the Indian international history of trademark law.
3. Define trademark and state the functions of trademark.
4. Explain the salient features of the Trademarks Act 1999.
5. Explain the Registerable and non-Registerable trademarks and check-out the significance of registration of trademark.
6. Explain the provision of infringement of trademark and distinguish it with passing off.
7. Discuss the evolution of concept of Trademark.
8. Discuss the powers and functions of the Registrar of Trademarks.
9. Discuss the evolution of concept of Trademark.
10. Analyse the legal importance of Trademark with essentials of a Trademark.
11. Explain the Registerable and non-Registerable trademarks and check-out the significance of registration of trademark.
12. Explain the provision of infringement of trademark and distinguish it with passing off.
13. Discuss the evolution of concept of Trademark.

Chapter 4

Cyber Intellectual Property

Cyber Intellectual Property

Introduction and overview of Cyber Intellectual Property; Intellectual property and cyberspace; Emergence of cybercrime; Grant in software patent and copyright in software; Software Piracy; Trademark issues related to domain names.

Information Technology Act-2002

Salient features of Information Technology Act, 2002; IPR provisions in IT Act; Internet policies of Government of India.

Data Protection

Data Protection in Cyberspace. **E-Governance**
E-E-Commerce. E-Contracts, Digital Signature.

Revision

Summary - Case law chart - Previous year question papers.

Introduction

The evolution of the digital age has significantly transformed the landscape of intellectual property (IP), leading to the inception and development of Cyber Intellectual Property (Cyber IP). In the digital age, the concept of intellectual property (IP) has expanded into the vast, interconnected realm of cyberspace. This term broadly refers to the application of traditional IP rights within the vast, interconnected expanse of cyberspace-a non-physical domain characterized by the exchange of data and communication across computer networks. The expansion of IP into this digital realm introduces both opportunities and challenges, particularly in safeguarding the rights of creators and innovators in an environment that is inherently anonymous and borderless. As the digital landscape continues to evolve, so too do the complexities of protecting intellectual creations in cyberspace.

Overview of Cyber IP

Cyber Intellectual Property (Cyber IP) encompasses the suite of legal rights and protections designed specifically for the digital realm, aimed at safeguarding creations that are inherently digital or are significantly manifested in digital formats. This includes a wide array of digital assets such as software programs, databases, websites, digital media (including music, videos, and text), and other forms of digital content that fuel the modern digital economy. The advent of Cyber IP represents a critical evolution in the field of intellectual property law, addressing the unique challenges and opportunities presented by the internet and digital technologies. By providing robust legal frameworks for the protection of digital creations, Cyber IP plays an indispensable role in promoting innovation, ensuring a level playing field in competitive markets, and securing the economic interests of creators who invest time, resources, and creativity into developing new digital products and services.

The core components of Cyber IP are designed to address various aspects of digital creation and use:

Copyright infringement: It is a statutory privilege granted by the government to inventors and to other persons deriving their rights from the inventor for fixed years to exclude other persons from manufacturing, using, or selling a patented product or processes.

The owner of a published artistic, literary, dramatic, or scientific work has copyright protection for that work to prevent someone else from using it in his own name for profit. is given.

Any use of this copyright without permission of the owner constitutes an infringement of this copyright. Making copies of software distributed on the Internet and sold by someone other than the owner is copyright infringement, as is copying his web pages or content on a blog.

In Shetland Times, Ltd. v. Jonathan Wills and Another, Wills is best known for his involvement in the notable lawsuit filed against him in 1996 as editor of The Shetland News website. Plaintiff in the case, The Shetland Times, has accused Wills' company, of infringing copyright by using hyperlinks that bypass his main Web site.

Software Piracy: Software piracy is the illegal use, copying, modification, distribution, sharing, or sale of computer software that is protected by copyright law. A software pirate is someone who intentionally or unintentionally engages in these illegal activities. You do not have to be a hacker to pirate software.

It is also subject to Indian copyright law. Knowingly using an infringing copy of a computer program on a computer; There are three types of copyright infringement:soft liftingsoftware counterfeitupload download.

Cybersquatting: The term cybersquatting deals with the illegal and the unauthorized registration and use of Internet domain names that are identical to trademarks, service marks, company names, or personal names. Cybersquatting through username infringement prevents brand owners from using known usernames and using their brands on this social media platform. Malicious reservations of usernames can also affect and undermine brand credibility.

Trademark Infringement: Trademark means a mark capable of being represented graphically and which can distinguish the goods or services of one person from those of other and may include shape of goods, their packaging and combination of colours (section 2 (zb) of Trademark Act, 1999). A trademark distinguishes one company product from other company. Once registered trademarks will be valid for 10 years and can be renewed any number of times for every 10 years.

E.g. Pepsi is a trademark of Pepsi Co for its cola drink, same way Coca Cola is a registered trademark of Coca cola Inc.

Geographical Indications: these are indications which identify a goods as originating in the territory of a member, or a region or locality in that territory, where a given quality, reputation, or other characteristics of the good is attributable to geographic region. The purpose of this identification is to protect customers from buying fake Geographically indications tagged product. Eg: Mysuru Silk Sarees: This tag is associated with Karnataka Silk Industries Corporation (KSIC), and one should use this tag other than KSIC.

Expanding the protections offered by Cyber IP is critical for the continued growth and dynamism of the digital economy. As digital technologies advance and permeate every facet of modern life, the importance of Cyber IP in protecting the rights of creators, fostering innovation, and supporting fair competition in the digital marketplace cannot be overstated. It not only incentivizes the creation of new digital content and technologies but also ensures that creators can reap the benefits of their inventions, contributing to economic growth and the enrichment of the digital commons.

Basic question on IPR in Cyberspace

How does one protect one's Intellectual Property Right and prevent its unauthorize use in the online medium?

Need for Protection of IP in Cyberspace

IPR gained tremendous significance in cyber space due to unprecedented advancement of computers and internet, growing e-commerce. A big challenge here is detection and protection of IPR in virtual space. Intellectual Property infringement to greater extent occur in the online medium. IP infringement in cyberspace is comprised of unauthorised or unlicensed use of trademark, tradenames, service marks, images, music, or sound reciting.

Intellectual property rights protect original works in the fields of art, literature, photography, writing, painting, as well as written choreography, audio, and video files. The IPR protects these works, both tangible and intangible. Increases market value - Intellectual property rights help generate business by licensing, selling, and even commercializing products and services protected by intellectual property rights. This improves market share and increases profits.

Intellectual property rights (IPR) and cyber law go hand in hand and need to protect online content. Cyberspace is the non-physical realm where computer-to-computer communication takes place over computer networks. With the advancement of technology, all individuals have the right to access cyberspace and share information.

In cyberspace, personal information may be shared by persons other than the owner. Therefore, your privacy is compromised. A person benefits from the creations of others. These rights are protected by his IPR. Patents, copyrights, trademarks, trade secrets, industrial and layout designs, geographical indications, etc. are intellectual property rights. If these rights are violated in cyberspace, there are various remedies available.

Challenges in protecting Cyber IP

The protection of Cyber IP is fraught with challenges that stem largely from the unique nature of the digital environment:

Anonymity of Users: The internet provides a level of anonymity that can complicate the process of identifying and taking legal action against infringers. This anonymity shields malicious actors, making it difficult to enforce IP rights effectively.

Global Jurisdictional Issues: The internet transcends geographical boundaries, leading to jurisdictional complexities. IP laws vary significantly from one country to another, making it challenging to pursue legal remedies across borders.

Rapid Replication and Distribution: Digital content can be copied and distributed across the globe instantaneously and at virtually no cost. This makes it exceptionally challenging to control the unauthorized dissemination of protected works.

Technological Advancements: The fast pace of technological change can outstrip the development of legal frameworks designed to protect IP. Innovations such as blockchain and artificial intelligence present new paradigms for creating and distributing content, requiring adaptive legal strategies.

Opportunities for protecting cyber-IP

Despite these challenges, the digital age also offers new tools and methodologies for protecting IP in cyberspace:

Digital Rights Management (DRM): DRM technologies help control the use of digital content at the user level, allowing rights holders to restrict copying, printing, and altering of their work.

Blockchain Technology: Blockchain can provide a tamper-proof, decentralized ledger for registering and verifying IP rights, offering a transparent and secure method for proving ownership and distribution rights.

International Cooperation: The global nature of the internet necessitates international collaboration in the enforcement of IP rights. Treaties such as the Agreement on Trade-Related Aspects of Intellectual Property Rights (TRIPS) and the efforts of the World Intellectual Property Organization (WIPO) aim to harmonize IP laws across borders.

Online Platforms' Policies: Major internet platforms have implemented policies and systems (such as YouTube's Content ID) to identify and manage copyright-protected material, providing rights holders with mechanisms to report and remove infringing content.

Universal Jurisdiction

Cyber disputes happen on cyberspace which is border less. Courts often base dilemma on exercising jurisdiction on the given case. The courts may assume jurisdiction for prosecuting a cyber offender based on universal jurisdiction, where the offensive acts are known universally by international law

Cybercrime

All activities done with criminal intent in cyberspace. It includes both criminal activities - conventional sense of activities newly evolved because of anonymous nature of internet. Increased use of cyberspace resulting in adding of new kinds of crime day by day.

There is no one exhaustive definition available for cybercrime, however, any activities which offend human sensibilities can also be included in its ambit. Cybercrime is any criminal activity involving a computer, connected device, or network.

Most cybercrime is aimed at profiting cybercriminals, but some cybercrime is committed to directly damaging or disable computers and devices. Others use computers and networks to spread malware, illegal information, images, or other materials. Some cybercriminals do both. H. Target a computer and infect it with a computer virus that infects other computers and entire networks.

The main impact of cybercrime is financial. Cybercrime includes several types of commercial criminal activities such as ransom ware attacks, email and web fraud, identity fraud, and attempts to steal financial account, credit card, or other payment card information. There is a possibility. Cybercriminals can target personal identities and corporate data to steal or resell. With many workers adapting to work-from-home routines due to the pandemic, the frequency of cybercrime is expected to increase in 2021, making protecting backup data especially important.

With the rise of Cyber IP, there has also been a surge in cybercrime targeting intellectual property. Cybercrime includes acts such as unauthorized access, use, reproduction, and distribution of digital content and software. This not only includes software piracy but also corporate espionage, hacking into databases to steal sensitive information, and the unauthorized use of trademarks online. The anonymity and borderless nature of the internet make it challenging to identify, prosecute, and deter cybercriminals.

Cybercrime encompasses a broad range of criminal activities that are carried out using computers, networks, and the internet. As technology evolves, so do the methods by which cybercrimes are committed. Below are some of the primary types of cybercrime, each targeting different aspects of the digital and physical world.

1. Hacking

Hacking involves unauthorized access to or manipulation of computer systems, networks, or websites. It can range from benign exploration to malicious activities such as stealing sensitive data, damaging systems, or distributing malware.

2. Phishing

Phishing is a deceptive practice where cybercriminals send fraudulent communications, often emails, that appear to come from a reputable source. The goal is to trick individuals into revealing personal information, such as passwords and credit card numbers.

3. Identity Theft

Identity theft involves unlawfully obtaining and using another person's personal data in some way that involves fraud or deception, typically for economic gain. This can include opening credit accounts, applying for loans, or making purchases under the victim's name.

4. Malware

Malware, short for "malicious software," includes viruses, worms, Trojans, ransomware, and spyware. These are designed to damage, disrupt, or gain unauthorized access to computer systems. Ransomware, a notable subtype, encrypts the victim's files and demands payment for their release.

5. DDoS Attacks

Distributed Denial of Service (DDoS) attacks aim to overwhelm a website or online service with traffic from multiple sources, making it unavailable to users. These attacks can be motivated by vandalism, activism, or extortion.

6. Cyberstalking and Harassment

This involves using the internet or other electronic means to stalk or harass an individual or group. Cyberstalking may include false accusations, monitoring, threats, identity theft, and data destruction or manipulation.

7. Fraud and Financial Crimes

Cybercriminals use various online methods to commit fraud and theft, including credit card fraud, electronic funds transfer fraud, and investment fraud. These crimes involve deceiving victims or financial institutions to gain money unlawfully.

8. Intellectual Property Theft

This includes piracy (the unauthorized copying, distribution, or use of copyrighted material) and theft of trade secrets or patented technology. Intellectual property theft can result in significant financial losses for creators and businesses.

9. Cyberespionage

Cyberespionage involves hacking into systems to steal sensitive information from governments, organizations, or individuals, often for political, military, or economic advantage.

10. Cyberterrorism

Cyberterrorism refers to the use of the internet to conduct violent acts that threaten or cause fear in society. This can involve attacking critical infrastructure, spreading propaganda, or disrupting services on a large scale.

11. Exploitation of Children

This category includes crimes such as the production, distribution, or possession of child pornography, as well as online grooming and cyberbullying targeting minors.

Grants in Software Patent and Copyright in Software

The intersection of software development and intellectual property rights has been a complex and evolving area of law worldwide. Two primary forms of legal protection available for software are patents and copyrights, each serving different aspects of software protection and having distinct requirements, scope, and duration. Understanding how grants in software patents and copyrights in software function is crucial for developers, businesses, and legal professionals navigating the digital landscape.

Software Patents

A software patent is granted to an inventor of a unique software innovation, offering exclusive rights to prevent others from making, using, selling, or distributing the patented invention without permission. The criteria and the extent to which software can be patented vary significantly across jurisdictions.

Key Aspects of Software Patents:

Eligibility: For software to be patentable, it generally must fulfill certain criteria, such as novelty, non-obviousness, and industrial applicability. It must represent a new solution to a technical problem.

Protection Scope: The protection afforded by a software patent is often specific to the particular method or process the software utilizes to perform a function or achieve a result, rather than the software code itself.

Duration: Software patents typically last for 20 years from the filing date, after which the patented technology enters the public domain.

Jurisdictional Variance: The United States, Europe, and Asia have different standards for what constitutes patentable software. For instance, the European Patent Office (EPO) has stricter criteria, requiring a software invention to have a "technical character" or solve a "technical problem" in a novel and non-obvious way.

Copyrights in Software

Copyright protection for software works is similar to copyright protection for literary and artistic works. It automatically protects the expression of ideas (i.e., the code) rather than the ideas, procedures, methods of operation, or mathematical concepts themselves.

Key Aspects of Copyrights in Software:

Automatic Protection: Copyright arises automatically upon creation of the software and does not require registration, although registration can provide significant legal advantages in enforcement and seeking damages.

Protection Scope: Copyright covers the specific code of the software (both source code and object code) and may extend to the user interface and documentation. It does not protect the underlying ideas, algorithms, procedures, or the functionality of the software.

Duration: Copyright protection lasts for the life of the author plus 70 years in most jurisdictions. For corporate authorship, the duration is typically 95 years from publication or 120 years from creation, whichever is shorter.

Global Coverage: Thanks to international treaties such as the Berne Convention, copyright protection is relatively uniform worldwide, providing a broad shield against unauthorized copying and distribution.

Distinguishing Between Patents and Copyrights in Software

What is Protected: Patents protect the functional aspects of a software invention (the "how" it does something), requiring a detailed disclosure of the invention. Copyrights protect the expression of ideas (the "what" is being expressed) in the code, without revealing the code itself.

Protection Process: Obtaining a patent is a complex, often costly process that involves a thorough examination of the invention's novelty and utility. Copyright, conversely, is automatic upon the creation of software, though registration can bolster legal protections.

Duration of Protection: Patents have a limited duration, after which the patented invention becomes public domain. Copyright offers a longer duration of protection, extending long after the author's death.

The dual framework of patents and copyrights in software offers creators comprehensive tools for protecting their intellectual property. While software patents can safeguard innovative functionalities and processes, copyrights protect the tangible expression of ideas in software coding. Navigating the intricacies of both legal protections requires careful consideration of the nature of the software being developed and the strategic goals of the creator or business. As the digital and technological landscape continues to evolve, so will the laws and regulations govern software patents and copyrights, underscoring the importance of staying informed and vigilant in protecting software innovations.

Software Piracy

Software piracy is the unauthorized copying, distribution, or use of software. It is a pervasive issue in cyberspace, affecting both large and small software developers. Piracy not only results in significant financial losses but also undermines the incentive structure that encourages innovation and creativity in software development.

Software piracy is the illegal copying, distribution, modification, sale, or use of proprietary software. So, briefly, software piracy is the act of stealing legitimate software by illegal means. Software piracy refers to the illegal copying and use of legitimate software. And now this critical problem has become a global problem. Software piracy regulations: Software piracy is illegal, and there are strict laws governing this illegal activity. So, law violators who break these copyright laws and cause copyright infringement are also fined. An End User License Agreement (EULA) is a license agreement primarily used to protect the legality of software. It is a contract between the manufacturer and the end user. This regulation defines legal software rules. A general rule of EULAs is to prevent users from sharing software with others. Types of Software Piracy: There are five main types of software piracy. Each type of software piracy is discussed in more detail below:

1. **Soft Lifting** - This is the most common type of software piracy. In this piracy, he is the single rightful owner of the software, but there are multiple users. For example, someone buys the original software and someone else downloads it onto their computer and uses it illegally. For example, we often borrow a colleague's software and install a copy of it on our computer. This is to save the cost of soft lifting certain types of software piracy.

2. **Disk Loader** - This is the most common type of software piracy, mostly seen at his PC stores. Shopkeepers purchase legal copies of software and replicate copies on multiple computers by installing them. In most cases, the customer/PC user is unaware of these things and is getting pirated software at her original S/W price or cheaper than the original price. This is a form of commercial software piracy.

3. **Counterfeiting** - is making copies of genuine/legal software programs that look like the real thing. This duplicate software is then sold out at low prices.

4. **Client-Server Overuse** - Client/server overload causes more copies of software to be installed than licensed. This is primarily the case when local departments work under local departments and install software on all computers for use by many employees, which is not permitted.

5. **Online Privacy** - Online privacy involves obtaining illegal software from online auction sites or blogs. This is done primarily through his P2P (Peer to Peer) file sharing system. It is often referred to as Internet piracy because it is obtained over the Internet.

Cyber Intellectual Property represents a critical area of law and policy that seeks to balance the rights of creators with the interests of the public in the digital age. As technology continues to evolve, so will the challenges and opportunities in protecting IP in cyberspace. The effective management of Cyber IP requires not only robust legal frameworks but also international cooperation and innovative approaches to enforcement and dispute resolution. As we navigate the complexities of the digital domain, the continued evolution of Cyber IP will be essential for fostering innovation, protecting creators, and ensuring the fair use of digital content.

Cybercrime's scope and scale continue to grow with technological advances, requiring constant vigilance, innovative cybersecurity measures, and legal frameworks to protect individuals, organizations, and governments from these evolving threats. Collaboration across borders and sectors is crucial in combating cybercrime effectively.

Internet Service Provider

An Internet Service Provider (ISP) is a company that provides individuals, businesses, and organizations with internet access and related services. These services can include web hosting, email hosting, and domain registration, among others. ISPs play a crucial role in connecting users to the internet, enabling the exchange of data through the vast network of networks that constitute the World Wide Web. The scope of services offered by ISPs can vary widely, ranging from basic dial-up internet access to high-speed broadband, fiber-optic connections, and wireless internet services.

Key Functions of ISPs:

Access Provisioning: ISPs are primarily responsible for providing users access to the internet. This can be through various means such as cable, DSL (Digital Subscriber Line), fiber-optics, satellite, and wireless connections.

Data Transmission: They facilitate the transmission of data over the internet, ensuring that users can send and receive data efficiently and securely.

Domain Name Services: Many ISPs offer domain name registration and hosting services, enabling users to establish their online presence with unique web addresses.

Email Hosting: Providing email services is another common function of ISPs, allowing users to have one or more email accounts associated with their domain.

Security Services: ISPs often provide security services, including firewalls, anti-virus protection, and spam filtering, to protect users from online threats.

Support Services: Customer support for troubleshooting and resolving connectivity issues is an essential service provided by ISPs.

Key ISPs in India:

India's internet landscape is served by a mix of state-owned and private ISPs, offering a range of internet services from basic dial-up to high-speed broadband. Here are some of the key ISPs in India:

- **Bharat Sanchar Nigam Limited (BSNL):** A state-owned telecom service provider, BSNL is one of the largest and oldest ISPs in India, offering a wide range of services across the country, including broadband, fiber, and wireless internet.

- **Reliance Jio Infocomm Limited:** A subsidiary of Reliance Industries, Jio has rapidly become one of the leading ISPs in India, known for its high-speed 4G LTE internet services and fiber-to-the-home (FTTH) broadband service, JioFiber.

- **Bharti Airtel Limited:** Airtel is one of India's leading private sector ISPs, providing a broad spectrum of internet services, including mobile broadband, Airtel Xstream Fiber broadband, and satellite internet.

- **Vodafone Idea Limited (Vi):** Resulting from the merger of Vodafone India and Idea Cellular, Vi is a major player in the mobile broadband sector, offering 4G internet services across India.

- **Tata Communications Limited:** Part of the Tata Group, Tata Communications offers a range of internet services, including broadband and internet leasing, primarily targeting the enterprise segment.

- **ACT (Atria Convergence Technologies) Fibernet:** ACT Fibernet is one of India's leading fiber broadband ISPs, known for its high-speed internet services in several major cities and towns.

- **Hathway Cable & Datacom:** Hathway is another prominent ISP in India, offering cable broadband services in various parts of the country, known for its high-speed internet packages.

The ISP landscape in India is characterized by intense competition, especially with the advent of affordable high-speed internet services. This competition has significantly benefited consumers, leading to improvements in service quality, coverage, and affordability of internet access across the country. As digital technologies continue to evolve, ISPs will play an increasingly central role in enabling access to digital services and content, further shaping the digital future of India.

Information Technology Act, 2000

The advent of the Internet has brought about momentous changes in our lives. People from all occupations are increasingly using computers to create, transmit, and store information in electronic form instead of traditional paper and documents. Information stored in electronic form has many advantages. It is cheap, easy to store, easy to search, and fast to connect. It has many advantages, but many have been exploited to gain themselves, harm, or harm others. Connectivity has resulted in many crimes and these increased crimes have led to the need for legal protection. Some countries are very vigilant and are enacting laws to govern the Internet. In response to the generational change, the Indian parliament has passed the Information Technology Act, 2000. The IT Law 2000 was designed based on the Model Law of the United Nations Commission on International Trade Law (UNCITRAL).

Advances in computer technology led to the Information Technology Act of 2000. The transformation of paperwork into electronic records and the storage of electronic data has changed the country's scenario significantly. The Act further amends the Indian Criminal Code, 1860, the Evidence Act, 1872, the Bankers' Book Evidence Act, 1891 and the Reserve Bank of India Act, 1934.

The Information Technology Act, 2000 (also known as the IT Act) is a law proposed by the Indian Parliament and notified to the United Nations General Assembly on 17 October 2000 by resolution of 30 January 1997. This is the most important law. It deals with cybercrime and e-commerce in India.

The primary purpose of this law is to conduct legal and trustworthy electronic, digital, and online transactions to mitigate or reduce cybercrime. The IT Act consists of thirteen chapters and 90 sections. The last four sections, beginning with "Section 91 - Section 94", deal with the amendments to the Indian Penal Code, 1860.

Salient features of the Information Technology Act, 2000

The Information Technology Act, 2000, encompasses several salient features:

1. **Definition and Penalties:** The Act defines cybercrime and prescribes specific penalties for offenses committed in cyberspace.

2. **Controller of Certifying Authorities:** Mandates the formation of a Controller of Certifying Authorities responsible for issuing and regulating digital signatures.

3. **Cyber Appellate Tribunal:** Establishes a Cyber Appellate Tribunal to address disputes arising from cyber law.

4. **Cyber Regulatory Advisory Committee:** Constitutes a Cyber Regulatory Advisory Committee to advise the Central Government on cybercrime and technological advancements.

5. **Amendments to Related Laws:** Proposes amendments to the Indian Penal Code, Evidence Act, Reserve Bank of India Act, and others to align them with the provisions of the IT Act.

6. **Facilitation of E-Commerce and E-Governance:** Acts as a facilitating law, promoting both e-commerce and e-governance.

7. **Enabling Electronic Records:** Serves as an enabling Act, providing legal recognition for electronic records and digital signatures.

8. **Regulation of Cybercrime:** Functions as a regulating Act, overseeing and regulating activities related to cybercrime.

9. **Recognition of Digital Gazette:** Recognizes the publication of the official Gazette in digital form.

10. **Foundation for Data Protection:** Lays the foundation for effective data protection in cyberspace.

11. **Adjudicating Officer:** Contains provisions related to the appointment of an adjudicating officer for dispute resolution.

12. **Appeal to High Court:** Appeals from the Cyber Appellate Tribunal lie with the High Court.

13. **Extraterritorial Applicability:** Applies to offenses committed outside India, asserting jurisdiction in cyberspace.

14. **Investigation by DSP Level Officer:** Specifies that investigations should be conducted by officers at the level of Deputy Superintendent of Police (DSP).

15. **Liability of Network Service Providers:** Network service providers are not held liable in certain cases.

16. **Corporate Offenses in Cyberspace:** Contains provisions addressing offenses committed by companies in the realm of cyberspace.

As part of being subscriber of United Nations commission on International Trade, which is formed to promote the harmonization and unification of international trade, so to remove unnecessary obstacles to international trade, India started harmonization efforts in Information Technology area.

In 1996, model law on e-commerce adopted followed by in 2000, Information Technology Act, 2000 enacted and it is applicable to whole of India. It is amended in 2008 to incorporate a section on Cyber Terrorism.

IT Act, 2000 is a primary law deals with cybercrime and eCommerce in India.

Data Protection in Cyber Space

The term data protection has become synonymous with the rights of citizens guaranteed by the state. With the beginning of the 21st century, the development of technology has increased significantly and has since become an integral part of human life. Today, these technologies are deeply connected to people's daily lives, so they contain important data related to users. This is why data protection has become so relevant to protecting personal interests.

The personal data may also be recorded by the website. As par to being subscriber of United Nations commission on International Trade, which is formed to promote the harmonization and unification of international trade, so to remove unnecessary obstacles to international trade, India started harmonization efforts in Information Technology area.

In 1996, model law on e-commerce adopted followed by in 2000, Information Technology Act, 2000 enacted, and it is applicable to whole of India. It is amended in 2008 to incorporate section on Cyber Terrorism IT Act, 2000 is a primary law deals with cybercrime and eCommerce in India.

Need of Data Protection

With the constant development of artificial intelligence (AI), many software applications such as Facebook, Google, etc. have been developed that can not only collect and store users' personal data, but also process the data for other purposes. increase. In 2018, the Cambridge Analytica lawsuit brought the protection of citizens' personal data to the attention of many states. Countries that have implemented different privacy policies, such as the European Council's GDPR (General Data Protection Regulation), Brazil's Brazilian Internet Act 2014, and Canada's Personal Data Protection and Electronic Data Protection Act (PIPEDA) There are about eighty countries in the world. and protect the personal data of citizens. This substantial number of countries reflects many states' concerns about the security of their citizens' personal data. Therefore, the implementation of various laws around the world includes data protection as one area of cyber law.

Data protection protects information from loss due to backup and restore. Data security refers specifically to the measures taken to protect the integrity of the data itself from tampering and malware. Provides protection against internal and external threats. Data protection is about controlling access to data.

Data Protection and General Data Protection Regulations (GDPR)

Most recently, GDPR was implemented by the European Council (EU) in 2018 and is considered one of the strictest laws to protect people's personal data in the European Union. This regulation has proven to be an important development in the field of data protection law. The implementation of this regulation has had a significant impact on major technology companies such as Google, Facebook, and many e-commerce websites. The regulation has certainly created new case law in the field of cyber law. The implementation of GDPR has taken the whole area of data protection rights to the next level. Let's briefly discuss some of its features that make this regulation far superior to others around the world.

Right to erasure – Under the GDPR, data subjects have the right to erasure their data after it has been stored in a data controller or processor.

Right to data portability - Under the GDPR, data subjects have the right to portability of their personal data from one data controller or processor to another.

E-Commerce

E-commerce, short for electronic commerce, refers to the buying and selling of goods or services using the internet, and the transfer of money and data to execute these transactions. E-commerce has revolutionized the way businesses operate, offering both opportunities and challenges. Here's a brief overview of key aspects of e-commerce:

Types of E-commerce Models

- **B2C (Business to Consumer):** This is the most common e-commerce model, where businesses sell directly to the final consumer. Examples include online retailers like Amazon and eBay.

- **B2B (Business to Business):** This model involves transactions between businesses, such as a manufacturer and a wholesaler, or a wholesaler and a retailer. Alibaba is a notable example.

- **C2C (Consumer to Consumer):** Platforms like eBay and Craigslist facilitate transactions between consumers, allowing individuals to sell directly to each other.

- **C2B (Consumer to Business):** In this model, individuals offer products or services to businesses, reversing the traditional business-to-consumer model. Freelance platforms like Upwork exemplify C2B e-commerce.

Advantages of E-commerce

- **Convenience:** E-commerce allows consumers to shop anytime, anywhere, enhancing shopping convenience.

- **Broader Reach:** Businesses can reach a global audience, breaking geographical limitations.

- **Cost Reduction:** E-commerce can reduce the cost of managing and processing inventory, allowing businesses to offer competitive prices.
- **Personalization and Customer Data:** Online platforms can track customer preferences and buying habits, enabling personalized marketing and improved customer experiences.

Challenges of E-commerce

- **Security Concerns:** The risk of data breaches and cyberattacks requires robust security measures to protect consumer data.
- **Intense Competition:** The low barrier to entry in e-commerce means businesses face intense competition, both from local and international players.
- **Logistical Challenges:** Managing supply chains and ensuring timely delivery can be complex, especially for international orders.
- **Return and Refund Policies:** Handling returns and refunds efficiently can be challenging but is crucial for customer satisfaction.

Future Trends in E-commerce

- **Mobile Commerce:** With increasing smartphone penetration, mobile commerce or m-commerce is becoming increasingly significant.
- **AI and Machine Learning:** These technologies are being used to personalize shopping experiences, manage inventory, and predict trends.
- **Social Commerce:** Selling directly through social media platforms is becoming more prevalent, integrating e-commerce into social experiences.
- **Sustainable Practices:** Consumers are increasingly favoring businesses that demonstrate environmental responsibility.

E-commerce has become an integral part of the global economy, continuously evolving with technological advancements and changing consumer behaviors. It offers vast opportunities for businesses to grow and reach new markets but also requires them to adapt to its challenges, particularly in areas like digital security, customer experience, and logistics. As e-commerce continues to evolve, staying informed and agile will be key for businesses looking to succeed in this dynamic landscape.

Legal aspects of e-Commerce in India

In 1996, model law on e-commerce adopted followed by in 2000, Information Technology Act, 2000 enacted, and it is applicable to whole of India. It is amended in 2008 to incorporate section on Cyber Terrorism IT Act, 2000 is a primary law deals with cybercrime and eCommerce in India.

Some key legal aspects of eCommerce in India included:

Information Technology Act, 2000 (IT Act): The IT Act is a comprehensive legislation that provides legal recognition for transactions carried out through electronic means including ecommerce, eContracts, digital signatures and cyber crimes

Consumer Protection Act, 2019: The Consumer Protection Act, 2019 and The Consumer Protection(E-commerce) Rules, 2000 introduced provisions to protect the rights of consumers in eCommerce transactions. It includes provisions related to product liability, unfair trade practices, and consumer grievances.

Goods and Services Tax (GST): eCommerce transactions are subject to GST in India. The GST law governs the taxation of goods and services, and eCommerce operators need to comply with GST regulations.

Foreign Direct Investment (FDI) Policy: FDI policy, especially in the retail sector, including eCommerce, has undergone changes. There were restrictions on FDI in inventory-based eCommerce, but 100% FDI was allowed in the marketplace-based model. It's essential to stay updated on any amendments to FDI policies.

Payment and Settlement Systems Act, 2007: This Act regulates payment systems and facilitates the development of electronic payments. It is relevant to eCommerce platforms in terms of online payment mechanisms.

Data Protection Laws: India was in the process of formulating a comprehensive data protection law. The Personal Data Protection Bill, 2019, was under consideration and aimed to regulate the processing of personal data in the country.

Competition Law: The Competition Act, 2002, deals with issues related to anti-competitive practices and the regulation of combinations. It is relevant to eCommerce, especially concerning issues like predatory pricing.

Intellectual Property Laws: Intellectual property laws, including trademarks and copyrights, are applicable to eCommerce platforms to protect against infringement.

E-Contract

E-contracts, or electronic contracts, are agreements created and signed in a digital format, existing entirely in an electronic environment. With the rise of e-commerce and the increasing digitization of business transactions, e-contracts have become a fundamental aspect of modern commerce, offering a convenient and efficient alternative to traditional paper-based contracts. Here's a comprehensive overview of e-contracts:

Definition and Nature

An e-contract is a legally binding agreement between parties to conduct a transaction electronically. These contracts are created, executed, and maintained in a digital format, utilizing electronic signatures to signify the agreement. E-contracts encompass a wide range of agreements, from simple clickwrap agreements seen on websites to complex contracts negotiated over email or specialized platforms.

Types of E-Contracts

- **Clickwrap Agreements:** These involve the user clicking a button or checking a box to indicate agreement to the terms, often seen during software installations or when signing up for online services.

- **Browse wrap Agreements:** Implied agreements where users agree to terms by merely using a website, with the terms accessible via a hyperlink, often found at the bottom of the page.

- **Shrink-wraps Agreements:** Terms are enclosed within a product's packaging, with opening the package signifying agreement. While more common in physical products, the concept extends to software licenses.

- **Email Contracts:** Agreements negotiated and agreed upon through email correspondence.

Advantages of E-Contracts

- **Efficiency:** E-contracts can be drafted, signed, and executed much faster than traditional contracts, saving time and resources.

- **Accessibility:** Parties can review and sign contracts from different locations, making transactions more convenient and faster.

- **Security:** Digital contracts can be encrypted and securely stored, reducing the risk of loss or damage.

- **Traceability:** Electronic contracts offer an audit trail, making it easier to verify actions and changes made to the document.

Challenges and Considerations

- **Authentication and Security:** Ensuring the identity of the parties and the security of the documents is crucial. Digital signatures and encryption are commonly used solutions.

- **Legal Jurisdiction:** The global nature of e-contracts can raise questions about which country's laws govern the contract.

- **Technical Issues:** Dependence on technology means that technical failures can potentially invalidate contracts or cause disputes.

Legal Validity

The legal validity of e-contracts is recognized in many jurisdictions around the world, thanks to laws and regulations specifically designed to facilitate electronic commerce. Legislation such as the Electronic Signatures in Global and National Commerce Act (E-SIGN Act) in the United States, the Electronic Communications Act in the UK, and the United Nations Commission on International Trade Law (UNCITRAL) Model Law on Electronic Commerce provides a legal framework that recognizes and enforces e-contracts, provided they meet certain criteria such as consent, intention, and consideration.

Legal aspects of eContracts in India

The legal validity of electronic contracts (e-contracts) in India is well-established and supported by various laws and legal provisions, making e-contracts as enforceable as their traditional paper-based counterparts. The foundation for this support comes primarily from the Information Technology (IT) Act, 2000, along with relevant provisions in the Indian Contract Act, 1872. Here's how these laws contribute to the legal framework governing e-contracts in India:

The IT Act, 2000, is landmark legislation that recognizes the validity of transactions carried out through electronic means. Key provisions related to e-contracts include:

Legal Recognition of Electronic Records and Signatures: Section 10A of the IT Act explicitly states that contracts formed through electronic means will not be deemed unenforceable solely because they are in electronic form. This section gives e-contracts the same legal standing as paper-based contracts.

Use of Digital Signatures: The Act provides for the legal recognition of digital signatures (now expanded to include electronic signatures), ensuring the authenticity and integrity of electronic documents. Sections

3, 4, and 5 detail how electronic records and signatures are to be attributed and treated under the law.

The Indian Contract Act, 1872, lays down the general principles of contract law in India. While it does not explicitly mention electronic contracts (being much older than the concept of e-commerce), its provisions are technology-neutral and sufficiently broad to encompass contracts made via electronic means. The essential elements of a valid contract under this Act-offer, acceptance, consideration, competent parties, legal purpose, and free consent-are applicable to e-contracts as well.

Evidence Act, 1872: Amendments to the Evidence Act have made electronic records admissible in court, provided certain conditions are met. This includes e-contracts, which can be presented as evidence in legal disputes.

RBI Guidelines: The Reserve Bank of India, which regulates financial institutions and transactions, has also issued guidelines that recognize and facilitate electronic banking transactions, indirectly supporting the framework for e-contracts involving financial transactions.

In summary, e-contracts are legally valid and enforceable in India, supported by a framework that integrates provisions from the IT Act, 2000, the Indian Contract Act, 1872, and other relevant legislation. As the digital economy continues to grow, the legal system in India is adapting to ensure that electronic transactions are facilitated in a secure and efficient manner, reflecting the evolving nature of business and commerce in the 21st century.

E-contracts represent a significant shift in how business transactions are conducted, offering efficiency and flexibility that traditional contracts cannot match. As technology continues to evolve and integrate into every aspect of business, the importance and utilization of e-contracts are expected to grow. Businesses and individuals engaging in electronic transactions should be aware of the legal frameworks governing e-contracts to ensure their agreements are valid, enforceable, and secure.

E-Governance

E-Governance, short for Electronic Governance, refers to the use of information technology (IT) and electronic communication tools in the delivery of government services, information, and communication to citizens, businesses, government employees, and other government entities. The goal of e-governance is to enhance the efficiency, transparency, and effectiveness of government processes, improve service delivery, and promote citizen participation in the decision-making process.

Key components of e-governance include:

Online Service Delivery: Providing government services and information through digital channels, such as websites and mobile applications, making it more convenient for citizens to access information and avail themselves of services.

Citizen Participation: Involving citizens in the decision-making process through online consultations, feedback mechanisms, and participation in various government initiatives, promoting transparency and accountability.

Digital Infrastructure: Building and maintaining the necessary IT infrastructure, including networks and databases, to support the delivery of electronic services and communication within government departments.

Government-to-Business (G2B): Facilitating interactions between government agencies and businesses, streamlining processes such as licensing, permits, and regulatory compliance through digital platforms.

Government-to-Employee (G2E): Enhancing internal government processes and communication among government employees through the use of digital tools, leading to increased efficiency.

Government-to-Government (G2G): Improving interactions and information sharing among different government departments and levels, reducing redundancy and enhancing coordination.

Data Security and Privacy: Ensuring the security and privacy of citizen information by implementing robust cybersecurity measures and data protection policies.

E-Governance aims to transform traditional government processes, making them more accessible, efficient, and responsive to the needs of the public. It plays a crucial role in modernizing administrative processes and fostering a more inclusive and participatory form of governance.

Digital Signature

Digital signatures offer a viable solution for creating legally enforceable documents Electronic records fill the gap by going completely paperless This eliminates the need to print documents for signature. Enable Digital Signature Alternative to time-consuming and expensive paper-based approval processes Fast, cheap, and fully digital. The purpose of a digital signature is to Like an autograph. Instead of using pen and paper, A digital signature uses a digital key (public key cryptography). like a pen In the paper method, digital signatures identify the signer Create a document and record a binding commitment to the document. But Unlike handwritten signatures, digital signatures are considered unforgeable.

Digital signatures can be easily transferred and cannot be imitated by others It can be automatically timestamped. Can use digital signature Any kind of message, whether encrypted or plaintext. very digital Signatures serve three functions:

- ⋏ Authentication - a digital signature is used to authenticate the source notice. Possession of a digital signature key is tied to a specific key A user; therefore, a valid signature indicates that the message was sent by him user.

- Integrity - In many scenarios, both senders and recipients of messages must be consistent. A guarantee that the message has not been modified in transit. Digital signatures use encrypted messages to provide this functionality Digest function.

- Non-Repudiation - A digital signature ensures that the sender knows who got it. If you sign information, you cannot later deny having signed it. Simply scanning your handwritten signature and digitally attaching it to your document is all you need. Not considered a digital signature. Ink signatures are easy to duplicate from one document to another by manually or electronically copying images.

A digital signature cryptographically binds an electronic ID to an electronic ID. Documents and digital signatures cannot be copied to another document. Digital signatures under the IT Act 2000 Digital signature means authentication of each electronic record by a subscriber according to an electronic procedure or procedure Provisions of Section 3. Section 3 describes the conditions to which electronic records may be subject. authenticated by attaching a digital signature of the reproduction specific steps. First, electronic records A mathematical function known as a "hash function" that freezes digitally An electronic record that ensures the integrity of the intended content Communications Contained in Electronic Records. Any tampering with the contents of the electronic record will immediately invalidate the digital signature.

Secondly, the identity of the person affixing the digital signature is authenticated through the use of a private key which attaches itself to the message digest and which can be verified by anybody who has the public key corresponding to such private key. This will enable anybody to verify whether the electronic record is retained intact or has been tampered with since it was so fixed with the digital signature. It will also enable a person who has a public key to identify the originator of the message.

'Hash function' means an algorithm mapping or translation of one sequence of bits into another, generally smaller, set known as "Hash Result" such that an electronic record yields the same hash result every time the algorithm is executed with the same electronic record as its input making it computationally infeasible to derive or reconstruct the original electronic record from the hash result produced by the algorithm; that two electronic records can produce the same hash result using the algorithm. Digital signatures are a means of ensuring the validity of electronic transactions.

Key Case Studies – Cyber Law

Case: National Association of Software and Service Companies vs Ajay Sood & Others,

In the case of National Association of Software and Service Companies (NASSCOM) vs. Ajay Sood & Others, NASSCOM, the plaintiff, sought legal action against defendants operating a placement agency involved in phishing. The defendants sent deceptive emails using NASSCOM's name to obtain personal data for headhunting purposes. The Delhi High Court, in its March 2005 decision, recognized phishing as an illegal act, issuing an injunction and allowing for the recovery of damages. Despite the absence of specific legislation on phishing, the court defined it as a misrepresentation causing confusion and harm. The judgment affirmed the protection of intellectual property rights, establishing that India recognizes and penalizes phishing under existing laws, reinforcing faith in the legal system for IP owners. The case highlights India's stance against phishing and reassures businesses of their ability to protect IP rights.

Case: Pune Citibank Mphasis Call Centre Fraud.

In the Pune Citibank Mphasis Call Centre Fraud case, ex-employees of Mphasis Call Centre, Pune, defrauded US Customers of Citibank, amounting to RS 1.5 crores, raising concerns about data protection. The unauthorized access to the electronic account space triggered the case as a cybercrime, falling under the purview of the Information Technology Act, 2000 (ITA-2000). The versatile nature of ITA-2000 allows for the inclusion of aspects not covered explicitly, incorporating IPC offenses committed with electronic documents. The judgment, under Section 66 and Section 43 of ITA-2000, holds the individuals liable for imprisonment, fines, and damages up to Rs 1 crore per victim, invoking the adjudication process for compensation.

Summary

- The evolution of the digital age has significantly transformed the landscape of intellectual property (IP), leading to the inception and development of Cyber Intellectual Property (Cyber IP).

- Cyber Intellectual Property (Cyber IP) encompasses the suite of legal rights and protections designed specifically for the digital realm, aimed at safeguarding creations that are inherently digital or are significantly manifested in digital formats.

- Cybercrime includes all activities done with criminal intent in cyberspace. It includes both criminal activities - conventional sense of activities newly evolved because of anonymous nature of internet. Activities such as Hacking, Phishing, Identity theft, Malware, DDoS attack, Cyberstalking, Fraud, IP theft, Cyberespionage, Cyberterrorism, and exploitation of children.

- Software piracy is the unauthorized copying, distribution, or use of software. It is a pervasive issue in cyberspace, affecting both large and small software developers.

- Advances in computer technology led to the Information Technology Act of 2000. The IT Law 2000 was designed based on the Model Law of the United Nations Commission on International Trade Law (UNCITRAL).

- E-commerce, short for electronic commerce, refers to the buying and selling of goods or services using the internet, and the transfer of money and data to execute these transactions. IT ACT, Consumer Protection Act, IPR Acts, GST Act etc. governs E-Commerce in India.

- E-contracts, or electronic contracts, are agreements created and signed in a digital format, existing entirely in an electronic environment. IT Act formalize the eContracts and digital signatures in India.

- Digital signatures offer a viable solution for creating legally enforceable documents. Electronic records fill the gap by going completely paperless. This eliminates the need to print documents for signature.

- E-Governance, short for Electronic Governance, refers to the use of information technology (IT) and electronic communication tools in the delivery of government services, information, and communication to citizens, businesses, government employees, and other government entities.

Questions

1. Critically analyze the issues relating to e-governance.
2. Classify Cyber Crimes and Categorize Cyber Criminals?
3. Examine the Legal Validity of e-contract in the light of the requirements of a valid contract as per the Contract Act and IT Act.
4. Explain the needs and advantages of e-taxation.
5. Discuss the various jurisdictional issues in Cyber Space.
6. Explain the various challenges faced for Cyber Crime Trials and Investigations.
7. Discuss the various Cyber Crimes related to Online Banking.
8. Explain Cyber Terrorism with suitable illustration.
9. Define E-Contract? Also discuss the provisions relating to E-Contract under the Information Technology Act 2000 and the issues involved in forming E-Contracts.
10. Critically explain with the help of decided case the information technology (Intermediary Guidelines) Rules, 2011.
11. Write short notes on following:
    i. Ethics and characters in Cyber space
    ii. Electronic records retention

iii. Data Protection

iv. Consumer Protection in Cyber World

v. Trans-national data flow

vi. Virtual banking operations

vii. Public key infrastructure

viii. Publication of Obscene material

ix. License to issue digital signature certificate.

x. (a) Electronic Signature (b) Online Payment Gateways (c) E-governance in India

xi. Pornography on the Internet

12. Write a brief note on classifications and Advantages of B2C E-Commerce and explain the challenges faced by it.

13. Explain the contractual obligations in Cyberspace.

14. Define the term 'Cyber Squatting' and what kinds of protection is available to the consumers in the Cyber World against it?

15. Define the term 'Online Contracts' and Explain the terms and conditions required for making 'Online contracts.

16. What is the necessity of Tax in Corporate finance and explain the regulations relating to corporate financial services?

17. Explain the historical background, Object, Extent, Scope, and Commencement of the Information Technology Act.

18. What is the liability of network service providers under the Act?

19. Explain about E-Governance under Indian Perspective.

20. Explain the powers of the Cyber Appellate Tribunal.

21. Define the term 'Hacking' and explain its essentials.

22. Discuss whether various International Treaties and Conventions have been instrumental in defining the path of intellectual property rights in the cyber world.

23. Explain the provisions for the protection of Online Trademarks under the Trademarks Act, 1999.

24. Describe the provisions of IPC applicable in Cybercrimes? Mention the various penalties imposed under the Information technology act?

25. Discuss the provisions relating to computer pornography in India.

26. What is electronic evidence? Explain the nature and admissibility of electronic records.

Chapter 5

Geographical Indications

Geographical Indications

Introduction and overview of Geographical Indications; Meaning and scope of GI; Important GIs of India and their features; Conflict between GI and Trademarks.

GI Act

Salient features of Protection of Geographical Indications Act; Protection of Geographical Indications; Misleading use of GI; Registration of GI; Right to use GI; Infringement; Remedies against infringement; Role and functions of Registrar of GI.

Summary - Case law chart - Previous year question papers.

Introduction to Geographical Indication

Geographical Indication is a sign that identifies a product as originating in each place. It states that a particular product belongs to a particular place. Since the qualities depend on the geographical place of origin there is a clear link between the product and its original place of production. Geographical Indication is primarily granted to agricultural, natural, manufactured, handcraft originating from a definite geographical territory. GI is an effective tool to protect the quality, reputation, or other character of goods attributable to their geographical origin. GI Tag provides similar IPR rights and protection to holders.

A Geographical Indication (GI) is an indication used for products that have a specific geographical origin and that have a quality, reputation, or characteristic inherently attributable to that origin. In India, GI tags are assigned by the Registrar of Geographical Indications (Chennai) under the Department of Industry and Internal Trade Promotion, Ministry of Commerce and Industry, Government of India.

India has a rich cultural and natural heritage and is home to a wide variety of products unique to certain regions. These products include handicrafts, textiles, agricultural products, food, and more. The GI label helps protect these products and their manufacturers by ensuring that only genuine products from a specific region are sold with that specific label. This helps to revitalize the local economy and preserve traditional knowledge and techniques.

As of 2021, there are over 380 registered GIs in India. Famous Indian GIs include Darjeeling Tea, Kashmir Pashmina, Kanchipuram Silk Saree, Alphonso Mango, Nagpur Orange, and Banarasi Silk Saree. These products are not only popular in India, but also internationally recognized and appreciated.

The GI label not only protects products from counterfeits, but also serves as a mark of quality and authenticity. By promoting products with the GI label, consumers can make informed choices and support the communities where the products are manufactured. As such, GI tags play a key role in promoting sustainable development and protecting cultural heritage.

Examples GI Tags

- Darjeeling Tea
- Bikaneri Bhujia
- Kashmiri Pashmina Shawl
- Agra Petta
- Kancheepuram Silks
- Mysore Silks
- Nagpur Orange

Art 1 (2) and 10 of the Paris convention for the protection of Industrial property, GIs are covered as elements of IPRs. GI also covered in Article 22 to 24 of TRIPS agreement.

Article 22 (1) indications which identify a good as originating in the territory of a member, or a region or locality in that territory, where a given quality, reputation, or other characteristic of the good is attributable to geographical origin.

India is also a member of World Trade Organization and TRIPS agreement. In India, GI are protected and governed by the Geographical Indication of Goods (Registration and Protection) Act,1999. It came into force with effect from 15th September 2003. Geographical Indication registry office is at Chennai.

Meaning and Scope of GI

A Geographical Indication (GI) is a type of intellectual property that indicates that a product originates from a particular geographic location and has a unique character, quality and reputation attributed to its origin. The Geographical Indication system in India is governed by the Geographical Indications of Goods (Registration and Protection) Act, 1999, which provides legal protection to products bearing the GI label.

The scope of GI protection in India is vast and covers a wide range of products including agricultural products, handicrafts, textiles, food, among others. and provide means to protect and promote these products in international markets.

A geographical indication system benefits both producers and consumers. Manufacturers of GI Mark products can benefit from legal protection against unauthorized use of product names and achieve the best prices on the market. Consumers benefit from assurance of authenticity and quality in the products they purchase. GI systems also promote local economic development, preserve traditional knowledge and techniques, and promote sustainable agricultural practices.

India has a rich cultural and natural heritage, and the geographical indication system has helped promote and maintain the diversity of its products. Some of his famous GI label products in India include Darjeeling Tea, Kanchipuram Silk Saree, Nagpur Orange, Alphonso Mango, and Banarasi Silk Saree. India's GI system is globally recognized, and GI tags have become an important marketing tool for promoting Indian products in international markets.

Important GIs of Indian and their features

Geographical Indications (GI) are signs used on products that have a specific geographical origin and possess qualities, reputation or characteristics that are attributable to that origin. India has a rich diversity of products, which are unique and are identified with a particular region or community. Here are some of the important GIs of India and their features:

1. **Darjeeling Tea** - This tea is grown in the Darjeeling district of West Bengal and has a distinctive aroma and flavor. The tea is light in color and has a floral fragrance.

2. **Kanchipuram Silk Sarees** - These sarees are made in the Kanchipuram district of Tamil Nadu and are known for their rich texture, intricate designs, and durability. They are usually made of pure silk and have Zari borders.

3. **Pashmina Shawls** - These shawls are made from the wool of the Pashmina goat, which is found in the Kashmir region of India. The wool is exceptionally fine and soft, making the shawls warm and luxurious.

4. **Banarasi Silk Sarees** - These sarees are made in the Varanasi district of Uttar Pradesh and are known for their intricate designs and heavy embroidery. They are made of pure silk and are often embellished with gold and silver threads.

5. **Alphonso Mangoes** - These mangoes are grown in the Konkan region of Maharashtra and are known for their sweet taste and fragrant aroma. They have a soft and pulpy texture and are often referred to as the "King of Mangoes."

6. **Basmati Rice** - This rice is grown in the foothills of the Himalayas in India and Pakistan. It is known for its long, slender grains and fragrant aroma. Basmati rice is often used in Indian and Middle Eastern cuisine.

7. **Nagpur Orange** - These oranges are grown in the Nagpur district of Maharashtra and are known for their sweet and juicy taste. They are often used to make orange juice and are also used in cooking.

8. **Blue Pottery of Jaipur** - This pottery is made in the Jaipur district of Rajasthan and is known for its unique blue and white designs. It is made using a special type of clay and is often used for decorative purposes.

These are just a few examples of the important GIs of India. There are many other products, including spices, handicrafts, and textiles, which are also recognized as GIs and are an important part of India's cultural heritage.

Following are the key GI Tags from the state of Karnataka.

#	Geographical Indication	Type	#	Geographical Indication	Type
1	Byadgi chilli	Agriculture	25	Monsooned Malabar Arabica Coffee	Agricultural
2	Kinnal Toys	Handicraft	26	Monsooned Malabar Robusta Coffee	Agricultural
3	Mysore Agarbathi	Manufactured	27	Coorg Green Cardamom	Agricultural
4	Bangalore Blue Grapes	Agriculture	28	Dharwad Pedha	Foodstuff
5	Mysore Pak	Sweets	29	Coorg Orange	Agricultural
6	Bangalore Rose Onion	Agriculture	30	Malabar Pepper	Agricultural
7	Coorg orange	Agriculture	31	Ganjifa Cards of Mysore	Handicraft
8	Mysore silk	Handicraft	32	Devanahalli Pomelo	Agricultural
9	Bidriware	Handicraft	33	Appemidi Mango	Agricultural
10	Channapatna Toys & Dolls	Handicraft	34	Kamalapur Red Banana	Agricultural
11	Mysore Rosewood Inlay	Handicraft	35	Sandur Lambani Embroidery	Handricrafts
12	Mysore Sandalwood Oil	Manufactured	36	Udupi Mattu Gulla Brinjal	Agricultural
13	Mysore Sandal Soap	Manufactured	37	Karnataka Bronzeware Logo	Handicraft
14	Kasuti Embroidery	Handicraft	38	Ganjifa Cards of Mysore Logo	Handicraft
15	Mysore Traditional Paintings	Handicraft	39	Navalgund Durries Logo	Handicraft
16	Mysore betel leaf	Agricultural	40	Guledgudd Khana	Handicraft
17	Nanjanagud Banana	Agricultural	41	Udupi Sarees	Handicraft
18	Mysore Jasmine	Agricultural	42	Mysore Silk Logo	Handicraft
19	Udupi Jasmine	Agricultural	43	Kolhapuri Chappal	Handicraft
20	Hadagali Jasmine	Agricultural	44	Coorg Arabica Coffee	Agricultural
21	Ilkal saree	Handicraft	45	Chikmagalur Arabica Coffee	Agricultural
22	Navalgund Durries	Handicraft	46	Bababudangiris Arabica Coffee	Agricultural
23	Karnataka Bronze Ware	Handicraft	47	Sirsi Supari	Agricultural
24	Molakalmuru Sarees	Handicraft	48	Gulbarga Tur Dal	Agricultural

Salient features of Protection of GI Act, India

The Geographical Indications of Goods (Registration and Protection) Act of India, often referred to as the GI Act, is a legal framework that provides protection to geographical indications (GIs) of goods in India. Geographical indications are indications that identify goods as originating from a particular territory, region, or locality where a given quality, reputation, or other characteristic of the goods is attributable to their geographical origin. Here are some of the salient features of the GI Act of India:

- Definition of Geographical Indication: The GI Act defines a geographical indication as any sign or symbol that is used to identify agricultural, natural, or manufactured goods as originating from a specific geographical area. It includes names of places, regions, or localities that are known for producing certain products.

- Registration and Protection: The GI Act provides for the registration of geographical indications. Once registered, the geographical indication is protected against unauthorized use, imitation, or misuse.

- Registrar of Geographical Indications: The Act establishes the office of the Registrar of Geographical Indications, responsible for maintaining the register of geographical indications and overseeing the registration process.

- Prohibition of Registration of Deceptive GIs: The Act prohibits the registration of a GI that contains or consists of a false or misleading indication or suggests that the goods originate from a different geographical region.

- Eligibility Criteria: To be eligible for registration, a geographical indication must satisfy certain criteria, including a link between the quality, reputation, or characteristics of the product and its place of origin.

- Rights of Registered Proprietor: The registered proprietor of a geographical indication has the exclusive right to use the GI and prevent others from using it without permission. This helps protect the reputation and distinctiveness of the product associated with GI.

- Duration of Protection: Geographical indications are protected for a period of ten years initially, and this protection can be renewed indefinitely for successive ten-year periods if the criteria for protection are met.

- Unauthorized Use Prohibited: The GI Act prohibits the unauthorized use of a registered geographical indication in a manner that misleads the public regarding the origin of the goods, or that constitutes unfair competition.

- Enforcement and Penalties: The Act provides for legal remedies and penalties for infringement of registered geographical indications, including injunctions, damages, and the seizure of infringing goods. Collective.

- ▲ Ownership: Geographical indications are often owned collectively by the producers or organizations representing the producers of the goods associated with the GI.

- ▲ Promotion and Development: The Act also encourages the promotion, development, and protection of geographical indications for the benefit of producers, consumers, and the geographical region itself.

- ▲ International Protection: India is a signatory to the Agreement on Trade-Related Aspects of Intellectual Property Rights (TRIPS) under the World Trade Organization (WTO), which provides for the protection of geographical indications. The GI Act aligns with international obligations.

- ▲ Assignment and Licensing of GIs: The Act provides for the assignment and licensing of registered GIs. The registered GI owner can assign or license the GI to another person for use in relation to the goods originating from the geographical region associated with the GI.

- ▲ Geographical Indications Registry: The GI Act established a Geographical Indications Registry in Chennai, which is responsible for receiving and processing applications for GI registration.

The GI Act of India is essential for safeguarding the unique identity and heritage of products associated with specific geographical regions and promoting their economic and cultural value. It helps protect consumers from deceptive practices while fostering the development of rural and local economies.

Benefits of Registration of GI

1. It provides legal protection to GI in India.
2. It prevents unauthorized use of a registered GI by others.
3. It in turn boosts exports.
4. It promotes economic prosperity of producers of goods produced in a geographical territory.
5. Rights conferred by registration are mentioned under section 21 of the action.

6. It rewards tradition and ensures knowledge is passed on to generations.

> **Basic question on IPR in Cyberspace**
>
> How does one protect one's Intellectual Property Right and prevent its unauthorize use in the online medium?

GI Trademark

Following are the key differences between GL and Trademark

Differentiator	Trademark	Geographical Indication
Scope	Distinguishes goods and services sold by **one producer.** E.g. TATA	Distinguishes goods and services sold by **group of producers.** E.g. Mysore silk owned by KSIC (Karnataka Silk Industries Corporation)
Source	Arises from Creative Genius	Existence of human and natural factors
History	No earlier recognition required to register	Recognition must exist for claiming GI
Nature	Monopoly right	Collective Public right
Purpose	Indicates who is the manufacturer of the product or services	Indicates the origin of the product
Assignment	Trademark can be assigned	GIs cannot be assigned
Timeline	It can be created overnight	It requires years to build recognition
Representation	It can be name, word, color, image, sound etc.	Geographical name

A trademark is a symbol used to identify and distinguish one entrepreneur's goods or services from another entrepreneur's goods or services, while a GI is a product that has a particular geographical origin and character, reputation, or character. is the symbol used for and is of this origin.

The dispute is that g.'s trademark is similar or identical to A. and is used on goods that do not belong to g. A. Relevant geographic regions. This can lead to consumer confusion and damage GI's reputation.

To address this issue, India enacted the Geographical Indications of Goods (Registration and Protection) Act, 1999 which provides for the registration and protection of geographical indications in India. The law prohibits the registration of trademarks that contain or consist of geographical indications or deceptive or misleading indications that suggest that goods originate from a particular geographical location.

A GI owner can claim infringement of her GI if the registered trademark is similar or identical to her GI in which it is registered, and the goods covered by the trademark do not originate from the geographical area associated with her GI. You can do.

In the event of a conflict between a geographical indication and a trademark, the geographical indication takes precedence as it is considered public property and represents the collective good will of the people associated with a particular geographical area. Its purpose is to prevent misappropriation of GI's goodwill using similar or identical brands.

In summary, trademarks and geographical indications serve different purposes but can cause disputes in India. However, India has introduced legislation to protect geographical indications and prevent them from being misused or abused using similar or identical trademarks.

Key Provisions of Geographical Indication Act, 1999

Sec 2 (e) - Definition of GI.

Sec 2 (g) - Types of goods are covered under the ambit of GI.

Sec 3-10 - Register and conditions for registrations.

Sec 11-19 - Registration.

Sec 20-24 - Effect of Registration

Sec 31-36 - Appeals to the Appellate Tribunal

Sec 37-54 - Offences, Penalties and Procedures

Key Definitions

Sec 2 (e): Definition of GI

"Geographical indication", in relation to goods, means an indication which identifies such goods as agricultural goods, natural goods or manufactured goods as originating, or manufactured in the territory of a country, or a region or locality in that territory, where a given quality, reputation or other characteristic of such goods is essentially attributable to its geographical origin and in case where such goods are manufactured goods one of the activities of either the production or of processing or preparation of the goods concerned takes place in such territory, region or locality, as the case may be.

Explanation - For the purposes of this clause, any name which is not the name of a country, region or locality of that country shall also be considered as the geographical indication if it relates to a specific geographical area and is used upon or in relation to particular goods originating from that country, region or locality, as the case may be; Sec 2 (f) defined goods "goods" means any agricultural, natural, or manufactured goods or any goods of handicraft or of industry and includes food stuff.

Sec 2 (g) defined indication

"Indication" includes any name, geographical or figurative representation or any combination of them conveying or suggesting the geographical origin of goods to which it applies.

The Register and Conditions for Registration (Sec 3 -10)

The Controller-General of Patents, Designs and Trademarks appointed under sub-section (1) of section 3 of the Trademarks Act, 1999, shall be the Registrar of Geographical Indications. (Sec -3)

The Central Government may appoint such officers with such designations as it thinks fit for the purpose of discharging, under the superintendence and direction of the Registrar, such functions of the Registrar under this Act, as he may from time to time authorize them to discharge.

The registrar can withdraw any matter pending with officers appointed under this act by giving reasons to concerned parties.

GI Registry will be established by central government. Presently it is located at Chennai, Tamil Nadu Register shall be maintained by the Registry for recording the registered Geographical indications with the names, addresses and descriptions of the proprietors, the names, addresses and descriptions of authorized users and such other matters relating to registered geographical indications as may be prescribed and such registers may be maintained wholly or partly on computer.

Following geographical indication are not permitted to registered under the act (Sec 9) -

1. The use of which would be likely to deceive or cause confusion; or
2. The use of which would be contrary to any law for the time being in force; or
3. Which comprises or contains scandalous or obscene matter; or
4. Which comprises or contains any matter likely to hurt the religious susceptibilities of any class or section of the citizens of India; or
5. Which would otherwise be disentitled to protection in a court; or
6. Which are determined to be generic names or indications of goods and are, therefore, not or ceased to be protected in their country of origin, or which have fallen into disuse in that country; or

7. Which, although true as to the territory, region, or locality in which the goods originate, but falsely represent to the persons that the goods originate in another territory, region, or locality shall not be registered as a geographical indication.

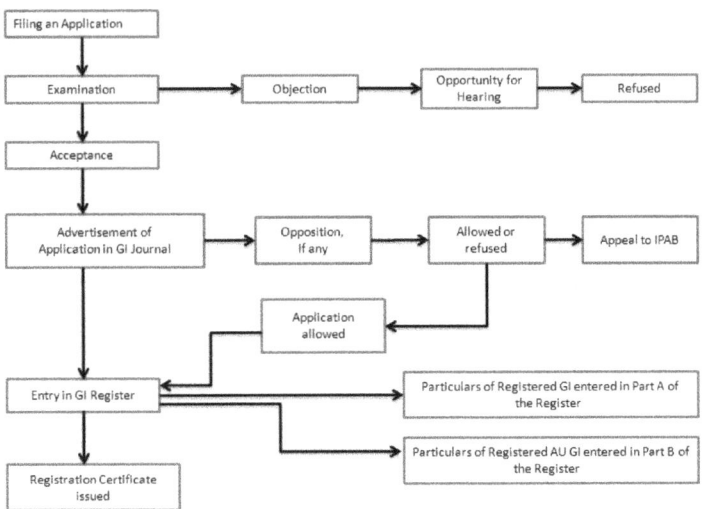

Registration (Sec 11 - 19)

Registration of Geographical Indications (GI) in India is governed by the Geographical Indications of Goods (Registration and Protection) Act, 1999. GI is a mark used for products that have a specific geographic origin and possess properties, reputations or characteristics that are inherently attributed to that origin.

Here are the steps to register a GI in India:

Filling of Application: The first step is to apply for registration of her GI at the Registrar of Geographical Indications in Chennai. Applications can be made by anyone who claims to be the owner of GI. Application review or Examination: Once the application is submitted, the Registry will check it to ensure that it meets the registration requirements. This includes checking whether the geographical indication is distinctive, whether the goods are identified as coming from a particular geographical area, and whether they have a good reputation based on their geographical origin. It is included.

Application Publishing: If the application is found to be suitable, it will be published in the Journal of Geographical Indications for three months. During this period, any person may object to the registration of a geographical indication.

Objection Hearing: If an objection is filed, the Registrar will consider the objection and hold a hearing to decide whether to register the geographical indication.

Registration of geographical indications: If no objection is filed or if the objection is dismissed, the geographical indication will be registered and a registration certificate will be issued to the geographical indication owner.

Once a GI is registered, it is protected against abuse and misuse. A GI owner can take legal action against anyone who uses her GI without consent.

Who can apply?
1. Any association of persons or producers or
2. Any organization or authority established by or
3. Under any law for the time being in force representing the interest of the producers of the concerned goods,

Who are desirous of registering a geographical indication in relation to such goods shall apply in writing to the Registrar in such form and in such manner and accompanied by such fees as may be prescribed for the registration of the geographical indication.

Application shall contain
1. A statement as to how the geographical indication serves to designate the goods as originating from the concerned territory of the country or region or locality in the country, as the case may be, in respect of specific quality, reputation or other characteristics of which are due exclusively or essentially to the geographical environment, with its inherent natural and human factors, and the production, processing or preparation of which takes place in such territory, region or locality, as the case may be;

2. The class of goods to which the geographical indication shall apply.

3. The geographical map of the territory of the country or region or locality in the country in which the goods originate or are being manufactured.

4. The particulars regarding the appearance of the geographical indication as to whether it is comprised of the words or figurative elements or both.

5. A statement containing such particulars of the producers of the concerned goods, if any, proposed to be initially registered with the registration of the geographical indication as may be prescribed; and

6. Such other particulars as may be prescribed.

Other Provisions

1. A Single application may be made for registration of a GI for different classes of goods and fee payable should be paid for each class of assets.

2. Application to be submitted to the office of Geographical Indication Registry within the territorial limits.

3. Every application shall be examined by the Registrar in such manner as may be prescribed.

4. The registrar may refuse the application or accept the application. In the case of refusal, the Registrar shall record in writing the grounds of refusal.

Provisions post submission of applications

1. The registrar may, after hearing the applicant if he so desires, withdraw the acceptance, and proceed as if the application had not been accepted.

2. Registrar shall advertise as per the procedure.

3. Any person can give notice in writing to the Registrar within 3 months with details of objection.

4. Once the object is reviewed, if the Registrar is satisfied with the application, shall issue the registration of GI to applicant and authorized users.

5. The Registrar may amend the register or a certificate of registration for the purpose of correcting a clerical error or an obvious mistake.

Duration, renewal, removal, and restoration of registration

1. The GI registration shall be for a period of 10 years.

2. Registrar shall send reminder notice before the expiry of the GI Tag to registered users.

3. If renewal is not done, registrar shall remove the GI from the registry.

4. One year grace period is available, during this period authorized user can apply for renewal.

Effect of Registration (Sec 20 - 24)

No person shall be entitled to institute any proceeding to prevent, or to recover damages for, the infringement of an unregistered geographical indication.

In all legal proceedings relating to a geographical indication the certificate of registration granted in this regard by the Registrar under this Act, being a copy of the entry in the register under the seal of the Geographical Indications Registry, shall be prima facie evidence of the validity thereof and be admissible in all courts and before the Appellate Board without further proof or production of the original.

Notwithstanding anything contained in any law for the time being in force, any right to a registered geographical indication shall not be the subject matter of assignment, transmission, licensing, pledge, mortgage or any such other agreement: Provided that on the death of an authorized user his right in a registered geographical indication shall devolve on his successor in title under the law for the time being in force.

Following are the rights of registered GI user (Sec-21)

1. Right to obtain relief in respect of the infringement of the geographical indication.

2. Exclusive right to use the geographical indication in relation to the goods in respect of which the geographical indication is registered, subject to conditions and limitations.

3. Where two or more people are authorized users of geographical indications, each of those persons has otherwise the same rights as against other persons as he would have if he were the sole authorized user.

Infringement of registered geographical indication (Sec-22)

Following acts are considered as infringement If unauthorized user.

a. Uses such geographical indication by any means in the designations or presentation of goods that indicates or suggests that such goods originate in a geographical area other than the proper place of origin of such goods in a manner which misleads the persons as to the geographical origin of such goods; or

b. Uses any geographical indication in such manner which constitutes an act of unfair competition including passing off in respect of registered geographical indication.

Appeals to the Appellate Tribunal (Sec 31 - 36)

Any person aggrieved by an order or decision of the Registrar under this Act, or the rules made thereunder, may prefer an appeal to the Appellate Board within three months from the date on which the order or decision sought to be appealed against is communicated to such person preferring the appeal.

No appeal shall be admitted if it is preferred after the expiry of the period specified under sub-section; Provided that an appeal may be admitted after the expiry of the period specified therefore, if the appellant satisfies the

Appellate Board that he had sufficient cause for not preferring the appeal within the specified period.

An appeal to the Appellate Board shall be in the prescribed form and shall be verified in the prescribed manner and shall be accompanied by a copy of the order or decision appealed against and such fees as may be prescribed.

No court or other authority shall have or be entitled to exercise any jurisdiction, powers, or authority in relation to the matters referred above.

The Registrar shall have the right to appear and be heard in any legal proceedings before the Appellate Board in which the relief sought includes alteration or rectification of the register or in which any question relating to the practice of the Geographical Indications Registry is raised.

The provisions of sub-sections (2), (3), (4), (5), (6) of section 84, section 87, section 92, section 95 and section 96 of the Trade Marks Act, 1999 (47 of 1999), shall apply to the Appellate Board in the discharge of its functions under this Act as they apply to it in the discharge of its functions under the Trade Marks Act, 1999.

In all proceedings under this Act before the Appellate Board the costs of the Registrar shall be in the discretion of the Board, but the Registrar shall not be ordered to pay the costs of any of the parties.

Offences, Penalties and Procedure (Sec 37 - 54)

Only authorized person or users can apply the geographical indication tag on the products (goods which are for sale which likely to lead to the belief that the goods in connection with which it is used are designated or described by that geographical indication. Unauthorized use or applying of GI tag by other than the authorized user amounts to Infringement.

Forms of Infringement

1. Use of GI by any means in the designation or presentation of goods which mislead the person as to the geographical origin of such goods.

2. Activity which constitutes an act of unfair competition including passing off.
3. Use of another GI tag to the goods.

Central government by notification can provide higher level of protection for certain products.

Penalty (Sec 38 - 44)

1. Penalty for applying false geographical indication.

   Unless he proves that he acted, without intent to defraud, be punishable with imprisonment for a term which shall not be less than six months, but which may extend to three years and with fine which shall not be less than fifty thousand rupees, but which may extend to two lakh rupees.

2. Penalty for selling goods to which false geographical indication is applied.

   Be punishable with imprisonment for a term which shall not be less than six months, but which may extend to three years and with fine which shall not be less than fifty thousand rupees, but which may extend to two lakh rupees.

3. Enhanced penalty on second or subsequent conviction.

   Again, convicted of any such offence shall be punishable for the second and for every subsequent offence, with imprisonment for a term which shall not be less than one year, but which may extend to three years and with fine which shall not be less than one lakh rupees, but which may extend to two lakh rupees:

4. Penalty for falsely representing a geographical indication as registered.

   They shall be punishable with imprisonment for a term which may extend to three years, or with fine, or with both.

5. Penalty for improperly describing a place of business as connected with the Geographical Indications Registry.

This shall be punishable with imprisonment for a term which may extend to two years, or with fine, or with both.

6. Penalty for falsification of entries in the register.

This shall be punishable with imprisonment for a term which may extend to two years, or with fine, or with both.

Other Provisions

1. In certain cases, use of GI by unauthorized user does not amounts to infringements -

a. If such act or omission is permitted under GI Act, or

b. If such an act or omission is permitted under any other law for the time being in force.

2. If the offence is prima-facie, then the court may order for forfeiture of goods where GI is applied without authorization. The accused can appeal against forfeiture orders also.

3. The following procedure is to be followed where invalidity of registration is pleaded by the accused.

a. If the court is satisfied that such defence is prima facie tenable, it shall not proceed with the charge but shall adjourn the proceeding for three months.

b. If the accused proves to the court that he has made such application within the time so limited or within such further time as the court may for sufficient cause allow, the further proceedings in the prosecution shall stand stayed till the disposal of such application for rectification.

c. If within a period of three months or within such extended time as may be allowed by the court the accused fails to apply to the Appellate Board for rectification of the register, the court shall proceed with the case as if the registration were valid.

4. No prosecution for an offence under this Act shall be commenced after the expiration of three years next after the commission of the

offence charged or two years after the discovery thereof by the prosecutor, whichever expiration first happens.

Remedies available to victim

Geographical Indication (GI) tags are a form of intellectual property protection granted to goods that have a specific geographical origin and possess qualities or a reputation that are attributable to that origin. The protection of GI tags is governed by the Geographical Indications of Goods (Registration and Protection) Act, 1999, in India. Under this act, civil and criminal remedies are available for the protection of GI tags in India. Here's a brief overview of these remedies:

Civil Remedies:

1. Injunction: A GI tag holder can seek an injunction from a court to stop any unauthorized use of their registered GI tag by third parties.
2. Damages: A GI tag holder can also claim damages from the infringer for any losses suffered due to the unauthorized use of their registered GI tag.
3. Account of profits: A GI tag holder can also seek an account of profits made by the infringer due to the unauthorized use of their registered GI tag.

Criminal Remedies:

1. Imprisonment: The act provides for imprisonment of up to three years and a fine of up to Rs. 2,00,000 for the offense of falsely applying a registered GI tag to any goods.
2. Seizure and forfeiture: The act also provides for the seizure and forfeiture of goods that are falsely labelled with a registered GI tag.

Overall, these civil and criminal remedies help to ensure that GI tags are protected, and any unauthorized use of registered GI tags is penalized.

Key Geographical Indication in India

Following are few GI in India

Darjeeling Tea: Grown in the Darjeeling district of West Bengal, this tea is renowned for its distinct flavor and aroma.

Basmati Rice: A variety of long-grain rice grown in the Indo-Gangetic plains, known for its fragrance and elongated grains.

Alphonso Mango: Grown primarily in the Ratnagiri, Sindhudurg, and other regions of Maharashtra, Alphonso Mango is famous for its sweetness and aroma.

Kanchipuram Silk Sarees: Traditional silk sarees from Kanchipuram in Tamil Nadu, known for their distinctive zari work and vibrant colors.

Banarasi Sarees and Brocades: Originating from Varanasi (Banaras) in Uttar Pradesh, these sarees are known for their intricate designs and use of fine silk and brocade.

Pochampally Ikat: Produced in Pochampally, Telangana, this handwoven fabric is known for its unique tie-and-dye technique.

Kolkata Rosogolla: A specific variety of the popular Indian sweet, Rosogolla, made in Kolkata, West Bengal.

Champagne: Although not Indian, it is worth noting that the name "Champagne" is a protected GI for sparkling wine produced in the Champagne region of France.

(Darjeeling Tea logo)	Darjeeling Tea Applicant: The Tea Board, a statutory authority of the GOI established under the Tea Act, 1953 Good: Agriculture Tea, State: West Bengal Type of Good: Tea grown in eighty-seven gardens within the district of Darjeeling
MysoreSilk heritage weaves 100% PURE SILK SINCE 1912 GI - 11	Mysore Silk Applicant: Karnataka Silk Industries Corporation Limited Goods: Handicraft State: Karnataka Type of Good: Raw Silk Yarn, Textile and Textiles Goods, Clothing (Sarees, readymade garments, ties etc.
Kanchipuram Silk	Kanchipuram Silk Applicant: State of Tamil Nadu Goods: Handicraft State: Tamil Nadu Type of Good: Silk Yarn, Saree

Rights of GI Right Holder

The right to use GI in India is granted to manufacturers and manufacturers who have registered their goods under the GI Act. The registration process involves submitting an application to the Register of Geographical Indications, certifying the origin of the product and showing that it has a particular character or reputation for that area.

Once registered, the geographical indication holder has the exclusive right to use the geographical indication in relation to the goods specified in the registration, allowing others to mislead consumers or mislead consumers as to the origin of the goods. Avoid using geographical indications in a confusing or confusing way. Registered her GI also provides legal protection against unauthorized use, imitation, or infringement by third parties.

It is important to note that the right to use geographical indications is not perpetual and must be renewed every ten years. In addition, registered GI holders are required to take initiative-taking steps to maintain product quality and reputation, failure to do so may result in revocation of registration.

Geographical Indication Registrar

The Geographical Indication Registrar (GI) of India is responsible for administering the Geographical Indications of Goods (Registration and Protection) Act, 1999. The main roles and functions of his GI Registrar in India are:

Registration of geographical indications: The Registrar is responsible for receiving and examining applications for registration of geographical indications in India. The registrar will review the application and decide whether to grant registration.

Publication of geographical indications: The Registrar publishes and publishes registered geographical indications in the Journal of Geographical Indications.

Grant and Refusal of Registration: Registrars are responsible for granting registrations to legitimate requests and denying registrations to those who do not meet the requirements of the GI Act.

Record Keeping: Registrars maintain a register of all geographical indications registered in India. This includes details of the owner, authorized users, and goods that the GI is registered for.

Protection and Enforcement: Registrars are responsible for protecting and enforcing the rights of registered geographical indication owners. Registrars may take legal action against those who abuse or violate the rights of registered GI holders.

Registration Update: The Registrar is responsible for renewing the registration of geographical indications every ten years upon receipt of renewal request and fee.

Promotion of geographical indications: Registrars promote awareness and importance of geographical indications in India through various means such as workshops, seminars and publications. Overall, the Registrar of Geographical Indications of India plays a key role in protecting and promoting the rights of holders of geographical indications registered in India.

Important Indian Case Laws of GI

There have been several important Indian case laws related to Geographical Indication (GI) that have helped in shaping the legal framework for GI protection in India. Some of the notable cases are:

- **Darjeeling Tea Association v. The Union of India (2002):** This case is one of the earliest and most significant cases related to GI protection in India. The Supreme Court of India held that Darjeeling tea is a geographical indication and granted legal protection to the term "Darjeeling" to ensure that only tea produced in the Darjeeling district of West Bengal could be marketed under that name.

- **TAHDCO v. S. Ram Reddy and Others (2002):** In this case, the Madras High Court held that GI protection can be granted to handicrafts and not just agricultural products. The court granted legal protection to the term "Kondapalli Toys," which are wooden toys made in the Kondapalli village of Andhra Pradesh.

- **Frooti Case (2006):** This case involved a dispute between two companies over the use of the term "mango drink." The Delhi High Court held that the term "mango drink" is a descriptive term and cannot be registered as a GI.

- **Pashmina Case (2010):** In this case, the Jammu and Kashmir High Court held that Pashmina is a GI and granted legal protection to the term "Pashmina" to ensure that only genuine Pashmina products from the Ladakh and Kashmir regions could be marketed under that name.

- **Basmati Rice Case (2021):** The Delhi High Court ruled in Favor of the Agricultural and Processed Food Products Export Development Authority (APEDA) and granted legal protection to the term "Basmati" to include certain regions of Madhya Pradesh and Uttar Pradesh. This case was significant as it expanded the geographic region for Basmati rice production and granted legal protection to the term "Basmati" as a GI.

These cases highlight the importance of GI protection and the need for a strong legal framework to prevent unauthorized use and exploitation of GIs, which can harm the interests of the producers and manufacturers associated with those products.

Summary

- Geographical Indication (GI) is an important form of intellectual property protection in India, recognizing that goods originate from a particular geographical region and have a particular character or reputation associated with that region. identify.

- The Geographical Indications Act provides registered geographical indication holders with legal protection and grants them the exclusive right to use geographical indications, allowing others to mislead consumers or mislead consumers about the origin of goods.

- Geographical Indication Registrar of India plays a significant role in administering the GI Act. This includes registering valid applications, extending registrations, maintaining registration of all her registered GIs, promoting recognition of GIs, and protecting and enforcing the rights of her registered GI holders.

- Overall, the Indian Geographical Indication System promotes and protects traditional knowledge, facilitates rural development, and contributes to the country's economic growth. It also helps protect the cultural and traditional heritage of different regions and communities in India.

Questions

1. What is the procedure for registering a Geographical Indication in India? Discuss the role of the Registrar of Geographical Indications in administering the GI Act.

2. Describe the legal framework for the protection of Geographical Indications in India.

3. What are the remedies available to registered GI owners in case of unauthorized use or infringement?

4. Analyse the significance of the "Coorg Orange" and "Mysore Silk" Geographical Indications in promoting the agricultural and textile sectors in Karnataka. What are the challenges faced in protecting and promoting GIs in the state?

5. Discuss the role of Geographical Indications in promoting rural development and sustainable agriculture practices in Karnataka. Give examples of some GIs that have contributed to the economic growth of the state. Explain the salient features of Geographical Indications (Registration and Protection) of Goods Act 1999.

6. Discuss the position of Geographical Indications under TRIPS agreement. (Trade Related Intellectual Property Rights).

7. Write note on 'Infringement of Regd. Geographical Indications.'

8. Which was the first Indian product to get the geographical indication tag?

9. Who issues GI tag in India?

10. Explain the concept of Geographical Indications (GI) in India and its importance in promoting traditional knowledge and cultural heritage. Give examples of some registered GIs in Karnataka.

Chapter 6

International Convention and Treaties

> **Introduction:** International covenants and Treaties – Historical development of IPR
>
> **Paris Convention:** Background, Governing Rules of Paris Convention – Nationality, Priority Treatment, and Country specific registration.
>
> **Patent Cooperation Treaty:** Background, Objectives of PCT; Salient features of PCT.
>
> **Madrid Convention:** Background, Salient features of Madrid Convention; International registration of marks.
>
> **WIPO:** Background, Salient features -WIPO; Organization of WIPO
>
> Summary - Case law chart - Previous year question papers.

Introduction

Intellectual Property Rights (IPR) protection has a rich and intricate history that spans numerous centuries. The inception of intellectual property rights dates back to 1474 when the Venetian government established a patent system to safeguard new inventions. However, it wasn't until the 19th century that the first international endeavors to protect intellectual property rights transpired.

Among the earliest international treaties on intellectual property is the Paris Convention for the Protection of Industrial Property, inked in 1883. This convention introduced the principle of national treatment, granting foreign patent and trademark applicants the same protection as domestic applicants in the countries that are signatories to the convention. The Paris Convention has undergone multiple amendments and presently encompasses various intellectual property rights, including patents, trademarks, designs, and geographical indications.

Throughout the 20th century, several other international treaties were established to safeguard intellectual property rights. The Berne Convention for the Protection of Literary and Artistic Works, forged in 1886, establishes minimum standards for copyright protection in signatory countries. The Universal Copyright Convention, signed in 1952, expanded upon the Berne Convention, providing a framework for copyright protection in countries not party to the Berne Convention.

The Agreement on Trade-Related Aspects of Intellectual Property Rights (TRIPS), signed in 1994 as part of the World Trade Organization (WTO) Agreement, stands as one of the most comprehensive international agreements on intellectual property rights. TRIPS sets minimum standards for the protection and enforcement of intellectual property rights in all WTO member countries, covering patents, trademarks, copyrights, and trade secrets.

In addition to these international treaties and agreements, many countries have enacted their own national laws and regulations to safeguard intellectual property rights. The evolution of IPR protection has been propelled by technological advancements, globalization, and the escalating significance of knowledge-based industries in the global economy.

The imperative for an international system to protect intellectual property emerged when foreign exhibitors declined participation in an international exhibition of inventions in Vienna in 1873. This catalyst led to the establishment of the Paris Convention for the Protection of Industrial Property in 1883, marking the inception of major international treaties. Various conventions and treaties instituted by the United Nations have aimed at enhancing the recognition of IPR in the modern world. Article 27 of the Universal Declaration on Human Rights (UDHR), 1948, addresses the importance of protecting intellectual property rights.

"Everyone has the right to freely participate in the cultural life of the community, to enjoy the arts and the share in scientific advancement and its benefit." The term scientific advancement is related to IPR.

Key International Treaties and conventions are: There are several key international treaties and conventions related to intellectual property rights (IPR), including:

1883: Paris Convention for the protection Industrial Property (Patent).

1886: Berne Convention for the protection of Literary and Artistic works (Copyright).

1891: Madrid Agreement concerning the International Registration of Marks.

1952: Universal Copyright Convention.

1967: WIPO Convention.

1970: Patent Cooperation Treaty (PCT).

1977: The Budapest Treaty on the International Recognition of the Deposit of Microorganisms.

1994: Trade Related Intellectual Property Rights (TRIPS).

2013: Marrakesh Agreement on transfer of books for people with blindness.

These treaties and conventions play a key role in providing a framework for the protection and enforcement of IPR on an international level.

Paris Convention - 1883

Paris Convention for the Protection of Industrial Property (1883): This convention introduced the concept of national treatment, ensuring that foreign applicants for patents and trademarks enjoy the same protections as domestic applicants in the countries that are signatories to the convention.

In response to the absence of adequate protection for inventions, inventors hesitated to disclose their innovations in public forums. Every inventor desires to reap the benefits of their creations, and a lack of proper protection can adversely affect innovation, research, and development. The Paris Convention, held in 1883, stands as the inaugural international convention in the realm of Intellectual Property Rights (IPR), with a particular focus on industrial property, especially patents.

The scope of the Paris Convention encompasses Industrial Property in the broadest sense, covering patents, trademarks, industrial designs, utility models, service marks, trade names, geographical indications, and the prevention of unfair competition.

Signed in Paris, France, on March 20th, 1883, the Paris Convention holds the distinction of being the first-ever intellectual property treaty. India became a member on December 7th, 1998, and the United States joined in 1887. Presently, the convention boasts 172 member countries. Both the Patent Cooperation Treaty (PCT) and the Trade-Related Aspects of Intellectual Property Rights (TRIPS) agreement draw upon the principles established in the Paris Convention. This historic convention laid the groundwork for robust and universally accepted regulations in the realm of intellectual property rights.

Three important decisions of Paris convention

Following are the three key decisions of Paris Convention

1. National Treatment
2. Right of Priority

3. Independence of Patent

National Treatment

According to the national treatment provisions, the Convention stipulates that, concerning the protection of industrial property, each Contracting State is obligated to extend the same level of protection to nationals of other Contracting States as it affords to its own nationals. Moreover, individuals from non-Contracting States are eligible for national treatment under the Convention if they are domiciled or possess a genuine and effective industrial or commercial establishment in a Contracting State.

Right of Priority

The Convention establishes the right of priority for patents (and utility models, where applicable), trademarks, and industrial designs. This right allows the applicant, based on an initial application filed in one of the Contracting States, to apply for protection in any other Contracting State within a specified period (12 months for patents and utility models; 6 months for industrial designs and trademarks). These subsequent applications are treated as if filed on the same day as the first application, giving them priority over applications filed by others during the relevant period for the same invention, utility model, trademark, or industrial design. Additionally, these subsequent applications, being derived from the first application, remain unaffected by events occurring in the interim, such as the publication of an invention or the sale of products bearing a trademark or featuring an industrial design. This provision provides practical advantages, allowing applicants seeking protection in multiple countries to decide within 6 or 12 months where they wish to seek protection and to carefully plan the necessary steps for securing such protection.

Independence of Patents

Patents granted in different Contracting States for the same invention are considered independent of each other. The grant of a patent in one Contracting State does not impose an obligation on other Contracting States to grant a patent. A patent cannot be refused, annulled, or terminated in any Contracting State based on actions taken in any other Contracting State.

The grant of a patent cannot be refused or invalidated on the grounds that the sale of the patented product or a product obtained through the patented process is subject to restrictions or limitations imposed by domestic law.

Each Contracting State may introduce legislative measures allowing for the grant of compulsory licenses to prevent abuses arising from the exclusive rights conferred by a patent, but only under specific conditions. Compulsory licenses, granted by a public authority of the concerned State and based on the failure to work or insufficient working of the patented invention, can only be issued upon a request filed after three years from the patent's grant or four years from the filing date of the patent application. The issuance of a compulsory license can be refused if the patentee provides legitimate reasons justifying their inaction. Furthermore, forfeiture of a patent is not allowed unless the grant of a compulsory license would be insufficient to prevent abuse. In such cases, proceedings for patent forfeiture may be initiated, but only after two years from the grant of the first compulsory license.

The Paris Union, as established by the Convention, comprises an Assembly and an Executive Committee. Every State that is a member of the Union and has adhered to at least the administrative and final provisions of the Stockholm Act (1967) is part of the Assembly. Members of the Executive Committee are elected from within the Union's membership, with the exception of Switzerland, which holds membership ex officio. The Assembly of the Paris Union is responsible for establishing the biennial program and budget of the WIPO Secretariat.

The Paris Convention, initially concluded in 1883, underwent revisions at Brussels in 1900, Washington in 1911, The Hague in 1925, London in 1934, Lisbon in 1958, and Stockholm in 1967, with subsequent amendments in 1979.

The Convention is open to all States, and instruments of ratification or accession must be deposited with the Director General of WIPO.

> **Compulsory Licensing**
>
> How does one protect one's Intellectual Property Right and prevent its unauthorize use in the online medium?

Today, the Paris Convention has 177 member countries and is administered by the World Intellectual Property Organization (WIPO). It has been revised several times over the years to keep pace with developments in technology and international trade. The most recent revision was adopted in 1979 and is known as the Stockholm Act.

Patent Cooperation Treaty (PCT)

The Patent Cooperation Treaty (PCT) is an international treaty signed in 1970 and entered into force in 1978. This agreement was created to simplify and streamline the process of applying for and obtaining patent protection for inventions in several countries.

Under the PCT, applicants can file a single international patent application with a single patent office, known as the "receiving office." This application will then be examined by an International Searching Authority, a prior art search will be conducted and an opinion on the patentability of the invention will be issued. The applicant can then "request" international preliminary examination, which includes a more detailed analysis of the patentability of the invention. After completion of the international phase, the application will be processed by the respective national or regional patent office for examination and grant of patent rights. The PCT system does not grant international patents. Rather, it provides a mechanism for filing and searching international applications and deferring the national/regional examination process.

The PCT system has many advantages for patent applicants, including:

Simplified process: Applicants may file a single international patent application instead of filing separate applications in multiple countries.

Research and testing: The international search and examination process provides valuable information about the patentability of an invention and helps applicants make informed decisions about whether to seek patent protection in a particular country.

Flexibility: The PCT system allows applicants to defer the decision of which country to file in and provides a longer time frame to enter the national/regional phase.

The PCT system is administered by the World Intellectual Property Organization (WIPO) and has 153 member countries as of 2021.

The Patent Cooperation Treaty was signed in Washington in 1970, came in force from 1978. Initially it was signed by eighteen countries as of 2018 members increased to 153 countries. Patent Cooperation Treaty is administered by World Intellectual Property Organization (WIPO).

With the PCT, a person can file one application in one language withing 12 months from the date of first application. This one application has the same legal effect as filing patent application in all the participating member countries. The PCT helps inventor to postpone the significant registration fees and processes required to be followed in each country.

Patents are territorially limited. Protect invention in multiple countries inventors, have a few options:

   a. Direct or Paris route: you can directly file separate patent applications at the same time in all of the countries in which you would like to protect your invention (for some countries, regional patents may be available) or, having filed in a Paris Convention country (one of the Member States of the Paris Convention for the Protection of Industrial Property), then file separate patent applications in other Paris Convention countries within 12 months from the filing date of that first patent application, giving you the benefit in all those countries of claiming the filing date of the first application (consult Question 11);

   b. PCT route: you can file an application under the PCT, directly or within the 12-month period provided for by the Paris Convention from the filing date of a first application, which has legal effect in all Contracting States of the PCT.

The PCT procedure includes:

Filing: you file an international application with a national or regional patent Office or WIPO, complying with the PCT formality requirements, in one language, and you pay one set of fees.

International Search: an "International Searching Authority" (ISA) (one of the world's major patent Offices) identifies the published patent documents and technical literature ("prior art") which may have an influence on whether your invention is patentable and establishes a written opinion on your invention's potential patentability.

International Publication: as soon as possible after the expiration of 18 months from the earliest filing date, the content of your international application is disclosed to the world.

Supplementary International Search (optional): a second ISA identifies, at your request, published documents which may not have been found by the first ISA which conducted the main search because of the diversity of prior art in different languages and different technical fields.

International Preliminary Examination (optional): one of the ISAs at your request, conducts an additional patentability analysis, usually on a version of your application which you have amended considering content of the written opinion.

National Phase: after the end of the PCT procedure, usually at 30 months from the earliest filing date of your initial application, from which you claim priority, you start to pursue the grant of your patents directly before the national (or regional) patent Offices of the countries in which you want to obtain them.

Intellectual Property Rights - 1

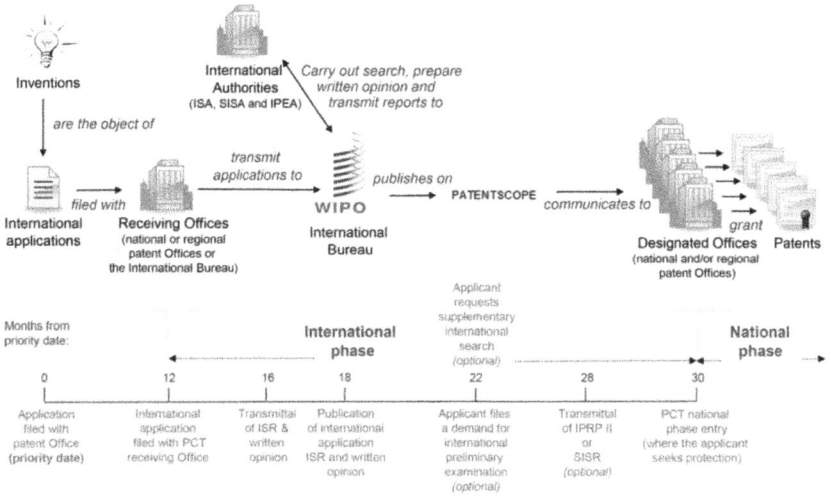

Source: www.wipo.org

Advantages of PCT

- The PCT offers the most efficient and cost-effective method for filing patent applications in multiple countries.
- It allows the filing of a single patent application with a single patent office in a single language, streamlined across each PCT country.
- The application undergoes a search by the international search authority.
- Formal examination of the international application is provided by an International Preliminary Examining Authority (IPEA).
- Centralized international publication of international patent applications is facilitated.
- By conducting searching and examination before entering the national phase, it reduces the workload on patent officers.

Objectives of PCT:

The national patent offices, promotes harmonization of patent law and procedure, and ensures that inventors from different countries are treated equally. The Patent Cooperation Treaty (PCT) is an international treaty that provides a uniform procedure for filing patent applications in multiple countries. The main objectives of the PCT are to:

One. Simplify the process of obtaining patents in multiple countries: The PCT allows inventors to file a single international patent application, which is examined by a central authority, an International Searching Authority (ISA) and an International Preliminary Examining Authority (IPEA). This process helps reduce the cost and time it takes to obtain patent protection in multiple countries.

Two. Promote international cooperation in patent matters: The PCT facilitates communication and cooperation between national patent offices, promotes harmonization of patent laws and procedures, and ensures that inventors are treated equally in different countries.

Three. To improve the quality of patent applications: The PCT provides a standardized process for filing patent applications and ensures that applications are complete and well-written. Reviews by the ISA and IPEA also help identify and correct deficiencies in the application.

Four. Give inventors a safe filing date: The PCT provides secure filing dates for international patent applications accepted by all member states. This date is important for determining the priority of inventions and protecting the rights of inventors.

Five. Give inventors time to evaluate the commercial viability of their invention: The PCT allows the inventor to decide in which countries to apply for patent protection within her 30 months from the priority date. This gives inventors time to assess the commercial viability of their inventions before incurring the costs of filing in multiple countries.

Madrid System

The Madrid System is a convenient and cost-effective solution for registering and managing trademarks globally.

A single international trademark application can be filed, and one set of fees paid for protection in up to 129 countries.

Trademark portfolio modifications, renewals, or expansions are managed through one centralized system.

The Madrid system, a result of the Madrid Agreement of 1891 and Madrid Protocol of 1989, simplifies trademark registration worldwide.

It is administered by the International Bureau of WIPO based in Geneva, Switzerland.

Process of applying Trademark under Madrid Agreement

The process of submitting an international trademark application through WIPO's Madrid System involves five fundamental steps:

Step-1: Complete your international trademark application.

Step-2: Submit the application to your Office of origin. (Warning: Do not send it to WIPO!) They will check that it corresponds to the particulars of your basic mark. The Office certifies the international application and sends it to us.

Step-3: Formal examination. We check that your international trademark application complies with all formal requirements (sufficient contact details, designation of at least one Madrid System member, quality of images, payment of fees, etc.). If it does not comply, we will send you and your Office of origin an 'irregularity notice' explaining how to correct the issue within a given time limit (typically three months). Sample irregularity notice PDF, Sample irregularity notice.

Step-4: We register your mark in the International Register, publish it in the WIPO Gazette of International Marks, send you a Certificate of Registration - acknowledgement of compliance with WIPO's formal requirements - and notify the designated members. Sample certificate of registration PDF, Sample Certificate of Registration.

Step-5: Substantive examination is conducted by the Office of each designated member. Each Office is required to either grant or refuse protection within a specified time limit- 12 months, or in certain instances, 18 months from the date on which we informed the Office of its designation.

Fees Payable for Trademark application processing under Madrid Agreement include.

A Basic Fee

- A complementary fee for each designated Madrid System member.
- A supplementary fee for each class of goods and services of more than three.

Benefits

1. Early brand recognition at Global level.
2. Cost effective.
3. Time Saving.
4. Single Application and will be in one language.

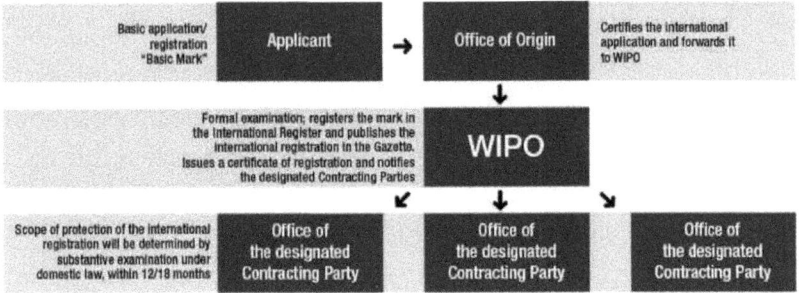

Source: www.wipo.org

World Intellectual Property Organization (WIPO)

WIPO was set up based on the Stockholm agreement which was signed in 1967 and came into force from 1970. WIPO head quarter is located at Geneva Switzerland. WIPO became one of the specialized bodies of UN in 1974. WIPO administers 26 international treaties and promotes the intellectual property at international level. India became member of WIPO on 1st May, 1975.

Major functions of WIPO are:

1. **Registration Activities:**

    Patents, Trademarks, and Designs: WIPO facilitates the international registration of patents, trademarks, and industrial designs. The organization provides a platform for applicants to seek protection for their intellectual property in multiple countries through simplified and streamlined processes.

    International Systems: WIPO manages international systems such as the Patent Cooperation Treaty (PCT) for patents, the Madrid System for trademarks, and the Hague System for industrial designs. These systems help applicants seek protection in multiple countries with a single application.

    Domain Names: WIPO also plays a role in resolving disputes related to domain names through the Uniform Domain-Name Dispute-Resolution Policy (UDRP), which provides a mechanism for the resolution of domain name disputes.

2. **Promotion of Inter-Governmental Cooperation:**

    Policy Development: WIPO fosters cooperation among its member states in developing and shaping intellectual property policies at the international level. This involves discussions, negotiations, and the formulation of agreements that harmonize IP standards and practices globally.

    International Treaties: The organization administers and facilitates the negotiation of international treaties, such as the Agreement on Trade-Related Aspects of Intellectual Property Rights (TRIPS), which establishes minimum standards for intellectual property protection within the World Trade Organization (WTO) framework.

3. Promotion of Sustainable Activities:

Technology Transfer: WIPO promotes the transfer of technology and knowledge, particularly in developing countries, to support sustainable development. This includes initiatives aimed at bridging the technological gap and fostering innovation.

Access to Knowledge: WIPO is involved in discussions about finding a balance between protecting intellectual property rights and ensuring access to knowledge, especially in areas such as public health and education.

4. Normative Activities - Setting up Norms and Standards:**

Development of Standards: WIPO engages in norm-setting activities by developing and promoting international norms, guidelines, and best practices related to intellectual property. This includes establishing standards for the protection of various forms of intellectual property like patents, trademarks, copyrights, and trade secrets.

Policy Guidance: WIPO provides policy guidance to member states, helping them align their national intellectual property laws and regulations with international standards.

5. Program Activities - Legal Technical Assistance and UN Initiatives:

Capacity Building: WIPO engages in legal and technical assistance programs to enhance the capacity of member states in managing intellectual property matters. This includes training programs, workshops, and other initiatives to strengthen the skills and knowledge of professionals in the field.

Collaboration with UN Initiatives: WIPO collaborates with other United Nations (UN) agencies and organizations on initiatives related to intellectual property protection. This can involve joint projects, research, and the integration of intellectual property considerations into broader development goals.

In summary, WIPO plays a multifaceted role in facilitating international cooperation, establishing norms, promoting sustainable activities, and providing legal and technical assistance to support the global intellectual property system. The organization's activities aim to strike a balance between fostering innovation and ensuring that the benefits of intellectual property contribute to sustainable development on a global scale.

Members of WIPO

The membership of the World Intellectual Property Organization (WIPO) includes various entities, and there are specific criteria for membership. Let's expand on the mentioned categories:

1. All the Members of the United Nations:

WIPO is a specialized agency of the United Nations (UN). As of January 2022, WIPO membership is open to all UN member states. This means that any country that is a member of the United Nations is eligible to become a member of WIPO.

There were 193 member states in the United Nations, and therefore, in principle, all these countries are eligible to become members of WIPO.

2. International Chief Justice Members:

There is no specific category of membership for "International Chief Justice Members" in WIPO. Membership is generally based on the status of a country as a United Nations member.

However, it's worth noting that WIPO's activities and services are relevant to legal professionals, including judges and justices who may be involved in intellectual property disputes.

3. General Assembly of WIPO by Invitation:

The General Assembly of WIPO comprises all member states, and participation in its sessions is generally open to all member states.

The General Assembly may also invite certain observers or non-member states to attend its sessions, allowing for broader participation in discussions on intellectual property matters. These invitations are typically extended based on the relevance of the issues being discussed and the desire for input from a diverse range of perspectives.

Representatives of intergovernmental organizations and non-governmental organizations (NGOs) may also be invited to participate as observers in WIPO's meetings and sessions.

General Assembly:

Composition: It is the highest decision-making body of WIPO and is composed of all member states.

Meetings: The General Assembly convenes at least twice a year to discuss and decide on key issues related to intellectual property and the functioning of WIPO.

Functions: It establishes the policies, approves the budget, and makes decisions on the overall direction of WIPO's activities.

WIPO Conference:

Frequency: This conference is held twice a year and plays a crucial role in finalizing the budget and other related activities of WIPO.

Decision-making: It provides a forum for member states to discuss and make decisions on various matters, including the organization's strategic priorities.

Coordination Committee:

Frequency: The Coordination Committee meets annually to address coordination issues within WIPO.

Functions: It focuses on ensuring effective coordination among the different components and bodies of WIPO, facilitating a harmonized approach to intellectual property matters.

International Bureau - Secretariat:

Location: The International Bureau serves as the Secretariat of WIPO and is located in Geneva, Switzerland.

Responsibilities: It is responsible for implementing the decisions made by the member states and the various WIPO bodies. The Secretariat supports the organization's day-to-day operations, manages administrative tasks, and facilitates communication among member states.

These organs collectively contribute to the governance, coordination, and implementation of WIPO's mission to promote and protect intellectual property worldwide. The General Assembly and WIPO Conference are crucial for policy decisions, while the Coordination Committee ensures efficient coordination, and the International Bureau acts as the administrative arm to execute the decisions and support the organization's activities.

Key Case Studies - International Conventions and Treaties

Following are few key case laws on International Conventions and Treaties:

- Legal Consequences of the Construction of a Wall in the Occupied Palestinian Territory (2004): The International Court of Justice (ICJ) issued an advisory opinion on the construction of a wall by Israel in the occupied Palestinian territory, emphasizing the illegality of the wall and its impact on the rights of the Palestinian population.

- Nicaragua v. United States (1986): In this case, the ICJ ruled on the United States' involvement in Nicaragua's internal affairs and its support for the Contras. The court found the United States guilty of unlawful use of force and ordered reparations to.

- Nicaragua. Prosecutor v. Tadić (1995): This case marked the establishment of the International Criminal Tribunal for the former Yugoslavia (ICTY). It clarified important legal principles concerning war crimes, crimes against humanity, and the jurisdiction of international criminal tribunals.

- The Paquet Habana (1900): This U.S. Supreme Court case recognized customary international law and affirmed that fishing vessels engaged in peaceful activities are exempt from capture as prizes of war.

- Prosecutor v. Jean-Paul Akayesu (1998): This case was the first international conviction for the crime of genocide. The International Criminal Tribunal for Rwanda (ICTR) found Akayesu, a former mayor in Rwanda, guilty of genocide and crimes against humanity during the 1994 Rwandan genocide.

- The Fur Seal Arbitration (1911): This arbitration settled a dispute between the United States and Great Britain over the hunting of fur seals in the Bering Sea. It established principles for the conservation and sustainable use of natural resources in international waters.

- Prosecutor v. Lubanga (2006): The International Criminal Court's (ICC) first trial, involving Thomas Lubanga, addressed the use of child soldiers in the Democratic Republic of Congo. This case highlighted the ICC's jurisdiction over war crimes, particularly the recruitment and use of child soldiers.

- Chorzow Factory (Germany v. Poland) (1928): In this case, the Permanent Court of International Justice (PCIJ) ruled on the consequences of Germany's violation of its obligations under international law during World War I and ordered reparations to Poland.

- Srebrenica Genocide Case (2007): The ICJ ruled on Bosnia and Herzegovina's genocide claims against Serbia, holding Serbia responsible for failing to prevent the genocide that occurred in Srebrenica in 1995.

- South China Sea Arbitration (2016): The Permanent Court of Arbitration delivered a ruling on a dispute between the Philippines and China regarding territorial claims and maritime rights in the South China Sea. The tribunal invalidated China's "nine-dash line" claim and clarified maritime entitlements under the United Nations Convention on the Law of the Sea.

Summary

- There are several important international agreements and conventions covering a wide range of issues aimed at promoting peace, human rights, environmental protection, trade, and intellectual property rights. Here is an overview of some important international agreements and conventions.

- Universal Declaration of Human Rights (UDHR): Adopted by the United Nations General Assembly in 1948, the Universal Declaration of Human Rights is a fundamental document that establishes a comprehensive range of civil, political, economic, social, and cultural rights. It has served as a common standard of practice for all countries and has influenced the subsequent development of human rights treaties.

- International Covenant on Civil and Political Rights (ICCPR): Enacted in 1966 and enforced in 1976, the ICCPR is a legally binding treaty designed to uphold and safeguard civil and political rights, encompassing the right to life, freedom of expression, freedom of religion, and the right to a fair trial. This treaty sets forth a structure for reporting and monitoring overseen by the United Nations Commission on Human Rights.

- International Covenant on Economic, Social and Cultural Rights (ICESCR): Also adopted in 1966 and into force in 1976, the ICESCR is a legal instrument that recognizes and protects economic, social and cultural rights such as the right to work, the right to education, the right to health and the right to a decent life. It is a binding treaty. Standard of living. It has established reporting and monitoring mechanisms through the United Nations Commission on Economic, Social and Cultural Rights.

- Paris Agreement: Adopted in 2015 as part of the United Nations Framework Convention on Climate Change (UNFCCC), the Paris Agreement aims to tackle climate change and keep global warming below 2 degrees Celsius above pre-industrial levels. It sets targets to reduce greenhouse gas emissions, promotes adaptation to the impacts of climate change, and provides a framework for international cooperation on climate issues.

▲ World Trade Organization (WTO): Established in 1995, the WTO is an international body concerned with global trade rules between nations. The aim is to ensure that transactions are as smooth, predictable, and free as possible. The WTO oversees various agreements on trade in goods, services, intellectual property, and dispute settlement mechanisms.

▲ WIPO Copyright Treaty (WCT) and WIPO Performances and Phonograms Treaty (WPPT): The WCT and WPPT, passed in 1996, are international treaties administered by the World Intellectual Property Organization (WIPO). It deals with copyright protection in the digital age and the rights of performers and record producers. These treaties set minimum standards for copyright protection and provide a framework for international intellectual property cooperation. These are just a few examples of the many existing international agreements and conventions. Each treaty focuses on a specific area of global interest and plays a key role in shaping international law, promoting cooperation, and addressing global challenges.

Questions

1. Explain the key objectives of the Madrid Convention for the International Registration of Marks. How does it facilitate the protection of trademarks globally?

2. Compare and contrast the Madrid Protocol and the Madrid Agreement under the Madrid System. Highlight the significant differences between the two.

3. Discuss the advantages and challenges for a business in utilizing the Madrid System for the international registration of trademarks. Provide examples to support your arguments.

4. What are the main principles and objectives of the Paris Convention for the Protection of Industrial Property? How does it

contribute to the harmonization of intellectual property rights internationally?

5. Explain the concept of "priority right" as established by the Paris Convention. How does it benefit inventors and creators in the process of obtaining patent protection?

6. Discuss the role of the Paris Convention in promoting fair competition and preventing unfair competition in the field of intellectual property. Provide examples to illustrate its impact.

7. Describe the purpose and functions of the Patent Cooperation Treaty (PCT). How does it simplify the process of filing international patent applications?

8. Discuss the significance of the international search and preliminary examination phases in the PCT system. How do these phases contribute to the patent application process?

9. Explain the role of the International Bureau of WIPO in the administration of the Patent Cooperation Treaty. How does it coordinate the international patent application procedure?

10. Provide an overview of the World Intellectual Property Organization (WIPO). How does WIPO contribute to the development and protection of intellectual property worldwide?

11. Discuss the services offered by WIPO in the field of dispute resolution related to intellectual property. Provide examples of cases where WIPO has played a crucial role.

12. Explain the role of WIPO in promoting and facilitating the international registration of trademarks, patents, and designs. How does WIPO support global innovation and creativity?

Bibliography

Bare Acts and International Treaties

1. Indian Patent Act (1970) - Legislation providing the legal framework for patents in India.

2. Indian Trade Marks Act (1999) - Legislation governing trademark registration and protection in India.

3. Information Technology (IT) Act (2000) - Indian legislation addressing various aspects of cyber laws, including cybersecurity.

4. Geographical Indications of Goods (Registration and Protection) Act (1999) - Legislation regulating the registration and protection of geographical indications in India.

5. Paris Agreement (2015) - International treaty under the United Nations Framework Convention on Climate Change (UNFCCC), in the context of India's commitment to environmental sustainability.

6. Patent Cooperation Treaty (PCT) - An international treaty allowing patent protection in multiple countries through a single application.

7. World Intellectual Property Organization (WIPO) publications - Global organization facilitating international cooperation in the field of intellectual property.

8. Madrid Agreement - The Madrid agreement is a convenient and cost-effective solution for registering and managing trademarks globally.

9. National Cyber Security Policy (2013) - Policy document outlining the strategic vision and framework for cybersecurity in India.

10. Intellectual Property Appellate Board (IPAB) rules and guidelines - Appellate body in India for hearing appeals against decisions of the Indian Patent Office and the Registrar of Trademarks.

11. World Trade Organization (WTO) publications - Global organization dealing with international trade and intellectual property agreements.

12. National IPR Policy (2016) - Policy document outlining the vision and strategy for intellectual property rights (IPR) in India.

13. Indian Copyright Act (1957) - Legislation governing copyright protection in India.

Books

1. Drahos, P., & Braithwaite, J. (2002). Information Feudalism: Who Owns the Knowledge Economy? Earthscan Publications.

2. Cornish, W. R. (2010). Intellectual Property: Patents, Copyright, Trade Marks, and Allied Rights. Sweet & Maxwell.

3. Kur, A. (2002). The Development of Intellectual Property Regimes in the Arabian Gulf States: Infidels at the Gates. Routledge.

4. Goldstein, P. (1994). Copyright's Highway: From Gutenberg to the Celestial Jukebox. Stanford University Press.

5. Ginarte, J. C., & Park, W. G. (1997). Determinants of Patent Rights: A Cross-National Study. Research Policy, 26(3), 283–301.

6. Merges, R. P., & Nelson, R. R. (1994). On the Complex Economics of Patent Scope. Columbia Law Review, 90(4), 839 – 916.

7. Chander, A., & Sunder, M. (2013). Intellectual Property: Private Rights, the Public Interest, and the Regulation of Creative Activity. Stanford University Press.

8. Basheer, S. (2017). The Case for Intellectual Property Rights: From a Liberal Perspective. Oxford University Press.

9. Raghavan, M. (2016). Intellectual Property Rights in the W.T.O. and Developing Countries. Oxford University Press.

10. Shamnad Basheer, S. (2015). Create, Copy, Disrupt: India's Intellectual Property Dilemmas. Oxford University Press.

11. Mukherjee, S., & Gupta, P. B. (2017). Intellectual Property Rights in India: Policy, Law, and Practice. Oxford University Press.

12. Bansal, A. (2013). Intellectual Property Rights: Unleashing the Knowledge Economy. PHI Learning Pvt. Ltd.

13. Birla, N. (2007). India and the Patent Wars: Pharmaceuticals in the New Intellectual Property Regime. Orient Blackswan.

14. Sen, S., & Basheer, S. (2014). Patent Law in India. LexisNexis India.

15. Chawla, R. (2016). Intellectual Property Rights: Text and Cases. PHI Learning Pvt. Ltd.

16. Goyal, R. (2019). Intellectual Property Rights: Indian and International Perspective. Pearson India Education Services Pvt. Ltd.

Websites

1. World Intellectual Property Organization (WIPO). (n.d.). Intellectual Property. Retrieved from https://www.wipo.int/about-ip/en/.

2. United States Patent and Trademark Office (USPTO). (n.d.). Types of Intellectual Property. Retrieved from https://www.uspto.gov/learning-and-resources/ip-policy/types-intellectual-property.

3. World Trade Organization (WTO). (n.d.). TRIPS Agreement. Retrieved from https://www.wto.org/english/tratop_e/trips_e/trips_e.htm.

4. Samuelson, P. (1994). The Copyright Grab. Wired, 2(03). Retrieved from https://www.wired.com/1994/03/copyright-2/.

5. https://lawbhoomi.com/
6. https://lextechsuite.com/
7. https://www.coursehero.com
8. https://corpbiz.io/
9. https://www.michiganlawyerhelp.com/
10. www.lexology.com
11. https://www.legislation.gov.uk/
12. https://indiankanoon.org/
13. https://www.legalserviceindia.com/
14. https://iprinn.com/
15. https://www.mondaq.com/
16. https://www.trademarksindia.net/
17. https://www.lawinsider.com/
18. https://jpassociates.co.in/
19. https://www.indiacode.nic.in/
20. https://ipindia.gov.in/
21. https://xpertslegal.com/
22. https://pib.gov.in/
23. https://www.casemine.com
24. https://www.icsi.edu/
25. https://globalregulatoryinsights.com
26. https://www.oregon.gov
27. www.brainly.com

www.ingramcontent.com/pod-product-compliance
Lightning Source LLC
LaVergne TN
LVHW061547070526
838199LV00077B/6933